Spending
Time
With God

A Teenager's Guide to Creating an Incredible Devotional Life

Mark Gilroy

Beacon Hill Press of Kansas City
Kansas City, Missouri

10   9   8   7   6   (1999)

To my six incredible children—
Lindsey, Merrick, Ashley, Caroline, Bo, and Zachary

They are daily reminders of God's goodness—
and why it's such a joy to spend time with Him.

Contents

Introduction

Discover the Power of Spending Time with God

I'm tired of trying to be a good Christian but always coming up short.

Sound familiar? Have you ever felt this way? Are you ready right now to discover an incredible new relationship with God? You've opened the right book.

A big part of the reason so many of us fall short in our Christian journey can be found in the word "trying." We really don't grow closer to God through *trying* harder, but we do grow closer to God through *trusting* more.

You can't tie apples to a telephone pole in your front yard and claim to have an apple tree—no matter how hard you try. Apple trees have a life force inside of them that began in a little seed.

In the same way, God is offering you a life force today. A power that begins inside of you. Your salvation, your daily walk with Jesus Christ, your deeper experience with the Holy Spirit—all are gifts from God's heart to yours.

No, you can't make yourself be a good Christian through your strongest efforts, no matter how diligent. But you do have a part in the process of growing closer to God.

Let's call it Spending Time with God. It's when you love and trust God so much that you completely turn your life over to Him. You put yourself in His hands and believe that He will transform you into the person you were always meant to be.

Wow.

Being close to the One who knows you best and loves you most. That's when you discover—and experience—the power of Spending Time with God. God begins to work in and through you in incredible ways.

As you read through the activities in this book, don't grit your teeth and tell yourself to try harder this time. Simply trust God more!

—Mark Gilroy

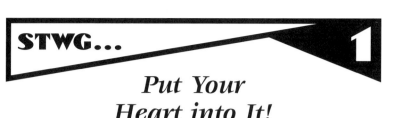

Put Your Heart into It!

Nothing great was ever achieved without enthusiasm.
—Ralph Waldo Emerson

▰▲▲▲▰

Do your best to improve your faith. You can do this by adding goodness, understanding, self-control, patience, devotion to God, concern for others, and love.
(2 Peter 1:5-7, CEV)

Whatever Happened to . . . ?

All of us lose touch with a special friend or neighbor at some time in our lives.

We move.

They move.

No more classes together.

They change.

We change.

You lose track of each other over the summer holiday, and—"it wasn't the same when she came back."

Whatever the reasons, we do lose touch. I wonder sometimes about the friends I went to school with in junior high, high school, and college. What are Wayne, Kris, Rob, Hugh, Mike, Sarah, Dan, Brett, Lori, Kenny, Lynne, Tim, Julie, and a whole bunch of other people up to these days? You can probably think of at least one person this

Carrie:

I used to just go to church because my parents made me. I really had a bad attitude. I didn't pay attention to the pastor or anything. Then one of my friends got really, really saved. She was so excited about serving God. That's all she talked about. I caught the same spirit from hanging around with her. I started thinking about everything Jesus did for me, and I started really feeling His love in my heart for the first time. I love Jesus so much now. It's the greatest feeling in the world! I'm a new person. I really am. Now I can't wait to get into God's Word. I feel as if I pray all day. And I love going to church. Sometimes my parents can't believe I'm the same person. Sometimes I can't believe I'm the same person. It's incredible!

9

very minute that you wonder about from time to time. Whatever happened to . . . ?

It's hard to keep relationships alive with all the friends you've ever had. If you've moved a lot, you know how easy it is to lose track of even your closest friends—the ones you hated to leave and promised never to forget.

Even if you've never moved away from your friends, you have seen and felt similar losses. Think of all the summer camp romances you've experienced or witnessed. After sending out friends to see if the other is interested, a guy and a girl become a couple. They fall madly in love. There's talk of staying true-blue till the day they are married. Camp ends. There's a flurry of letter writing. E-mails burn up the wires between your computers. Phone calls are made at all hours of the day and night. Then . . .

Mom and Dad get the first phone bill. The calls are cut back quickly and significantly.

The letters slow to a trickle—"I wrote him over two weeks ago; he should have had a letter back by now!"

It's just not as fun to meet in cyberspace anymore.

The "beautiful" relationship is lost.

There is, of course, a reason that relationships get lost along the way. Relationships take time, effort, and nurturing. They don't just happen by accident. Maybe that's why our society is filled with so many divorces and fractured families. TV, books, magazines, and other media have emphasized feelings and romance plenty. All the work needed to make a marriage thrive and become something beautiful, however, gets left out and comes as a shock to many young couples.

I know that when I am away from home for more than one or two days, I have to work especially hard on my relationship with my wife and children. There is absolutely no doubt that I love them while I am away. They know that. But expressions of love and personal contact must be rekindled.

What About a Relationship with God?

You already know where this is going, don't you? A relationship with God is the same way. It, too, takes time, effort, care, and enthusiasm. Too often, though, we treat a relationship with God like something that is just going to happen whether or not we cultivate it or put our hearts into it.

We go to the altar, and voilà!—we're set for life. Right? Too many of us have stumbled and backslidden and have seen others stumble and backslide to believe that for even a minute. The bottom line is:

If you want a beautiful and dynamic relationship with God, you must spend time with Him. You have to put your heart into it! Nothing great—including a great spiritual life—is accomplished without enthusiasm.

That is what this book is about: spending time with God. How can you spend time with God in such a way that your relationship with Him will flourish and you will mature spiritually?

Basic Ways to Spend Time with God

Through this book, you are going to experience a variety of activities that will help you develop a pattern of spending time with God. You can spend time with God through . . .

- ▶ **Keeping a spiritual journal**
- ▶ **Praying**
- ▶ **Studying God's Word**
- ▶ **Worshiping and growing with other believers**
- ▶ **Ministering to others**
- ▶ **Sharing your faith with others**

These activities will do for your spiritual life what nourishment, training, rest, and oxygen do for the athlete. But instead of better physical health, coordination, and performance, it is your spiritual life that will be stronger and more joyful than ever before.

As you get started in these spiritual disciplines, you may not be able to sense God's presence very strongly at first. You may feel at times as if you are the only one who showed up for your time with God. Don't let that discourage you or tempt you to believe that God is not there. No vision or audible voice is promised. But through this book you will be provided with some simple how-tos that will help you discover God's presence in your life more and more as you make time for Him.

But I've tried all these ways before. Nothing seemed to happen. They didn't work for me.

If you turn on your TV set and you don't get a picture or any sound, what do you do? Do you conclude that there are no such things as television programs? Do you scrap the set? Or do you find out what is wrong with the set and have it fixed? (Hmmm. Let me see.) Obviously, you get the set fixed!

The activities listed above have helped Christians spend time with God for the last 2,000 years or so. They have been modified and adapted for different people at different times. But they have been constant means of growth. If they haven't worked for you, maybe something needs to be fine-tuned in your life. Perhaps there is some short circuit or wrong connection keeping you from clearly seeing God at work in your life.

Follow along with Jesus' parable about four soils and four hearts found in Mark 4:1-20 to be sure there are no obstacles hindering you from spending time with God. Through this evaluation, you will be able to ask yourself, "Have I really put my heart into it?"

Cultivating the Soil

In this parable, Jesus tells about a farmer who went out to plant seed. Some of the seed fell on . . .

1. Hard soil

In Jesus' day the road system was not developed as it is today. The existing roads got you in the general area you wanted to go, but after that you had to create your own shortcuts. This usually meant setting off across a farmer's field. After a number of people had taken the same shortcut, a hardened path began to form in the farmer's land. He would go out to plant, but the seed that fell on this hardened ground would only rest on the surface. The soil was too hard for the seed to penetrate.

One of the obstacles to spending time with God is like hard ground. We can call it a "hard heart." Like the hard soil that keeps out the seed, it is difficult for the presence of God to penetrate the life of a person who has a hard heart. There is a barrier he or she has put up that keeps God's Word from taking root.

Causes of a hard heart are . . .

- ◐ **Unbelief and doubt**—Like doubting Thomas, many struggle with the idea of spending time with a God they cannot see! They, too, want to touch their fingers to the nail-pierced hands and side of Jesus. Their motto is: *I'll believe it when I see it!*

- ◐ **Hurts and disappointments**—Some have been hurt enough times along the road of life that a part of them inside has seemed to die. *I don't want to be hurt again* is their motto. *When I open myself up to the love of others, I open myself up to be hurt again. It's safer not to try.*

- ◐ **Failure and sin**—Some have failed so many times: *I'm tired of getting close to God at a camp or retreat and not being able to live it when I go to school the next week,* that they fear opening their hearts. Better not to try at all than to look like a fool and fail again.

○ **Self-will and pride**—Some want control of their lives so much that there is no way they are going to let anyone else take charge. Their motto is simple: *I will live my life the way I want to.*

All of us are born with a hard heart—a built-in resistance to letting God have control. However, you probably would not be reading this book if you had not already allowed God to break through the barrier of sin that separated you from Him. Yet you may still have some hard spots and sections in your heart that will hinder your relationship with God. Can you think of some ways that your heart needs to be "tilled" and broken up right now—some doubts, some unresolved hurts, some past failures that need to be forgiven and forgotten? Write them down here and commit them to God's healing touch.

2. Rocky soil

The farmers of Jesus' day had a major battle working with rocky soil. The soil they farmed was fairly shallow, due to limestone deposits just beneath the surface. The shallow soil did not allow enough room for roots to take hold or for moisture to be present to nourish the plants. With this soil, the farmers had to dig out the rock if any crop was to grow there.

Rocky soil represents what we can call "shallow hearts." People with these hearts are easily swayed by friends and the group. There is not enough depth for them to develop roots and become strong and substantial Christians. These people are characterized by great, promising starts on whatever project they begin. But as time goes by, they lose interest and move on to something else. There is an initial commitment, but it's a shallow commitment.

How is your commitment to Jesus Christ right now? Is it wavering? Or have you made a firm decision to follow Jesus no matter what the cost? If you are wavering, why don't you write out a short prayer of commitment right now. If your decision is firm, write out a brief prayer expressing your desire to spend quality time with God.

3. Thorny soil

Some of the seed that the farmer planted fell in particularly thick patches of weeds. The seed took root, started to grow, but was choked out before it became a full-grown plant.

Another obstacle to spending time with God is found in a heart that is like thorny soil. We can call this heart the "crowded heart." With the person who has this heart, there is not the initial resistance to God's presence as there is in the life of the person with a hard heart. There is much excitement over being a Christian. But spending time with God quickly becomes only one of many things that need attention and take up time.

You understand this heart. It might very well be the biggest obstacle in your life and the lives of other teenagers. I asked 15 high school students one Sunday morning what is the number one hindrance in their lives to spending time with God. Thirteen said, TIME.

I want to have devotions, but by the end of the day, I am so tired that I don't feel like it. There are too many things going on in my life.

The major cause of a crowded heart is too much activity and a lack of solid priorities. There are so many good things to do that it is difficult to know what comes first. Spending time with God is important, but then, so are a lot of other things. . . .

Maybe you have struggled with finding time for God. Perhaps a "crowded heart" is a hindrance in your relationship with God. Are there some "weeds" that need to be pulled in your life? How might you have to reprioritize some aspects of your life if you are to truly put your heart into this relationship with God?

4. Fertile soil

There was also an amazingly fertile soil that had the capability of bringing about an enormous crop. Not only did the seed take root, but also it grew and blossomed and yielded an unbelievably productive harvest.

Fertile soil and receptive hearts are not just for a select few. A receptive heart is for you too. No matter what type of heart characterizes your life right now, no matter what obstacles stand in your way of spending quality time with God, you can have a "fertile heart." You can open your life to the full-ness of God.

The activities for spending time with God found in this book will help you discover ways to cultivate the soil of your heart.

Your Reactions and Actions

1. What activities in your life really motivate you? What would help you be more enthusiastic about your devotional life?

2. Read Ephesians 2:8-10. How will remembering the main message of these verses keep us from falling into spiritual pride?

3. Can you remember a time when you really felt God's pres-ence? What did it feel like? What made you more receptive to experiencing God at this moment in your life?

4. Write out a brief prayer, expressing to God your desire to spend time with Him.

2

Getting Started Now!

Heaven never helps the man who will not act.
—Sophocles

▮▲▲▲▮

Don't be fools; be wise: make the most of every opportunity you have for doing good. Don't act thoughtlessly, but try to find out and do whatever the Lord wants you to.
(Ephesians 5:15-17, TLB)

What's Wrong with Tomorrow?

You wake up with a stare. You look at your clock on the nightstand next to you and groan. You jump out of bed and run for the shower. You put on your clothes as fast as you can. You grab your books and run for the front door. You yell "bye" to your mom over your shoulder as you race for the bus stop.

You make it to the door just before the driver releases the clutch and pulls away. Your heart is racing, but you made it. The door hisses open, you climb the stairs, and you head for your regular seat on the bus.

But almost missing the bus isn't your real problem. You were supposed to get up two hours ago so you could study for the big test

John:
I always had trouble in school because I did everything at the last minute. I was getting a lot of Cs and Ds. My mom was pretty unhappy with me. What changed me was when I heard a sermon from my pastor on memorizing Scripture. I started doing it that night, and it's as if everything was suddenly different in my life. I didn't memorize verses to try to get better grades, but that's what happened. I'm getting all A's and Bs now. I feel as if a lot of things have improved in my life, including my relationship with my mom. Most of all, my relationship with God is better. I wish I had gotten serious about getting to know God sooner. But I'm not complaining, because I'm on the right track now.

in algebra. And algebra is first hour. That means you have 15 minutes in the bus and 7 minutes in homeroom to look through your book. That means no time to work a couple of practice problems. And that means you probably aren't going to do great on your algebra final exam.

Sound familiar? Maybe you've never suffered from the temptation to procrastinate. Most of us have! We've complained:

"There just aren't enough minutes in the day."

"If I could only get organized."

"I meant to, but then I forgot, and then it was too late."

"I just can't get motivated."

"I already have too much going on in my life."

"The hard part for me is getting started."

Some of us are even proud about procrastinating. We worry that if we make plans, get organized, and start getting things done on time, it would mean that life isn't fun anymore.

I'm just a creative and spontaneous kind of person. I do things when I feel like it.

The problem is that you don't always *feel* like getting ready for the upcoming algebra test.

How about a devotional life? Spending time with God? Growing closer to Him through prayer and Bible study? How long have you known it is important? How long have you put off getting started?

Maybe there's nothing wrong with tomorrow, but what's wrong with today?

Getting Started Now!

God told Moses to go back to Egypt to rescue his people *now* (Exodus 4:12).

David declared that he is a new man because *now* he has obeyed God's Word (Psalm 119:67).

Solomon tells his sons to pay attention to his wise words *now* if they want to live a successful life (Proverbs 5:7).

When God offers forgiveness of sins to the people of Israel, He says to consider what a great offer this is *now* (Isaiah 1:18).

The prophet Zechariah warns the people to turn from their wicked ways *now* if they want to escape judgment (1:4, KJV).

Paul tells us that *now* is the time to wake up—and put our salvation into practice (Romans 13:11).

You get the idea! *Now* is the day to begin spending time with God. Here are a few reminders to help you begin your journey today.

1. Don't forget how you got here.

It is probably safe to assume that the reason you are reading this book is that you have made a decision to follow Jesus Christ as your Lord and Savior—or you are seriously considering this response of faith. You now want to grow closer to Him and mature as a Christian.

There is a temptation that you can easily fall into at this point. You can come to the conclusion that *you* will be able to make yourself grow spiritually through these activities.

But just as you were saved by faith, you will continue to grow by faith alone. You cannot force growth to happen through your own strength. You will not become a stronger Christian solely through hard work and discipline. In other words, the activities listed in this book will not in and of themselves ensure that you will have a closer walk with God.

What will happen is that through discipline, and through using the activities of spending time with God discussed here, you will place yourself in a position to receive God's strengthening and nurturing into your life—if you exercise faith.

The farmer does all that he can to bring about a bountiful harvest of wheat or soybeans. He plows his soil. He plants seeds. He fertilizes. He times his work so that his crop will receive the right amount of sun and rain. However, he cannot make even one seed grow. Growth is a miracle of life found within the seed.

Don't forget that your Christian walk is by faith from first to last (Romans 1:17). By remembering this, you will not fall into the sin of pride.

2. Don't forget the reason for these activities.

My prayer is that as you read through this book, you will catch the excitement of actually spending time with God. The point is not just to fill out journals, memorize Scripture, do good things for people, and find other ways to keep busy. Doing the things in this book will put you in a position where you can grow, but that's not the primary goal. The goal is to spend time with God, not to do devotional activities.

Don't fall into the same trap as the ancient Israelites, who were very proficient at *acting* religious but who forgot the reason they were being religious.

In Hosea 6:6, God says, "I don't want your sacrifices—I want your love; I don't want your offerings—I want you to know me" (TLB).

3. Set reasonable goals.

John Wesley prayed two hours or more every morning. John Wesley changed his world. England was never the same after he rode his horse from town to town, preaching four or five times a day.

You, too, can make a difference in your world through developing a dynamic prayer life. However, you may not want to start off with a goal of praying for two hours every morning—or riding on horseback across your country to preach the gospel. (At least not until you finish high school.) You may want to begin with a goal of praying for five minutes every morning.

Likewise, it would be great if you could read the entire Bible this year. But you may want to begin by just trying to read the New Testament.

If you wrote in a spiritual journal every day for the next year, you would undoubtedly learn many things about yourself and how God is working in your life. But maybe you should begin by recording entries in a journal once or twice a week.

It would be easy to get so excited about spending time with God that you set yourself up for failure. You can easily set such lofty goals that even the Christian who has been at it for years could not accomplish. These activities for spending time with God will take practice and time. Why not set smaller goals that you know you can meet, and consider new goals in a month or two?

Here is a suggested time schedule if you are just getting started in devoting time to God every day:

- ▶ **Bible study**—*10 minutes per day*
- ▶ **Prayer**—*5 minutes per day*
- ▶ **Journaling (see chapter 3)**—*10 minutes on Sunday night and 10 minutes after school on Thursday*
- ▶ **Worship with other believers**—*Attend church services on Sunday; attend Wednesday night Bible study; get together with a friend from your teen group on Saturday*
- ▶ **Ministry and witness to others**—*Continue to watch and pray for opportunities to witness to a friend; help any visitors feel welcome at Wednesday night Bible study; tutor a student who is new to your community; mow the lawn of your next-door neighbor who isn't physically able to exert himself or herself anymore*

4. Be ready to change and grow.

When you spend time with God, He will change you and help you grow. You need to be warned that spending time with God is not for the timid. When Moses went up on Mount Sinai to receive the Ten Commandments, he prepared the people to witness the presence of God. Their terrified response to Moses was, "Speak to us yourself and we will listen. But do not have God speak to us or we will die" (Exodus 20:19).

Your devotional life will not always be comforting. It will not just make you feel better and more secure. Your time with God will also disturb you. You will be confronted with your strengths and weaknesses. Some of the times I spent with God when I was a teenager that still come to mind were some of the difficult times. They were times when I agonized over obedience or knowing what God wanted to do in my life. You will find it the same way.

Don't get me wrong. There are peace and comfort that come from spending time with God. However, don't get too comfortable. God will bring about changes in your life! So get ready to grow!

The Benefits of Journaling

One of the most valuable tools that you can use to aid you in your time with God is a spiritual journal. A journal provides you with an opportunity to record your thoughts and ideas during your time with God. The remaining chapters in this book explain how to use a journal to address the following dynamics of your spiritual walk:

▶ Spending Time with God . . . My Spiritual Journey
▶ Spending Time with God . . . My Time in Prayer
▶ Spending Time with God . . . My Time in God's Word
▶ Spending Time with God . . . My Time in Worship
▶ Spending Time with God . . . My Time in Ministry

You don't *have* to use a journal to spend time with God or to practice the activities taught in this book. However, I recommend it because it has been so helpful in my life and the lives of many others I know. You may already have a journal that you're planning to use to begin your journaling process. If so, great! If not, you can easily pick one up at your local bookstore. The next chapter contains more information on choosing a journal that's right for you.

The Joy of Spending Time with God Now

So will planning and organizing your devotional life rob you of spontaneity and joy? The words of Thomas Carlyle remind us that success is a result of solid planning and goals:

The man without a purpose is like a ship without a rudder. Have a purpose in life, and, having it, throw such strength of mind and muscle into your work as God has given you.

But it is King David who reminds us of the joy of Spending
Time with God:

> *Shout praises to the LORD, everyone on this earth.*
> *Be joyful and sing as you come in to worship the LORD!*
> *You know the LORD is God!*
> *He created us, and we belong to him;*
> > *we are his people, the sheep in his pasture.*
> *Be thankful and praise the LORD*
> > *as you enter his temple.*
> *The LORD is good!*
> > *His love and faithfulness will last forever.*

(Psalm 100, CEV)

Your Reactions and Actions

1. In what areas of your life are you most tempted to procrastinate?

2. Go ahead and make some personal goals for spending time
   with God. Why don't you fill in a schedule for the next five
   days:
   DAY ONE

   DAY TWO

   DAY THREE

   DAY FOUR

   DAY FIVE

3. Finish this sentence: Some things that the Lord wants to do
   in my life right now are . . .

... Through a Spiritual Journal

It is necessary to write, if the days are not to slip emptily by. How else, indeed, to clap the net over the butterfly of the moment? For the moment passes, it is forgotten; the mood is gone; life itself is gone.
—Vita Sackville-West

▲▲▲▲

Our LORD, I will remember the things you have done, your miracles of long ago. I will think about each one of your mighty deeds.
(Psalm 77:11-12, CEV)

Put It in Writing?

If you had a good friend who moved to another state, which would you prefer—a letter or a phone call? AT&T commercials used to claim that a phone call is the next best thing to being there. Perhaps the closest thing to being right next to each other today is having the same Internet service. Now you can jump into a chat room together or send instant messages and talk as long as you want —or until your parents tell you to hit the sack. Plus you get beeped when the other person comes on-line, so you know they are there.

But there's still something

Jamie:
I started keeping a journal last year when my parents were going through a divorce. I knew a lot of friends whose parents split up, but I didn't think it would ever happen in my family. I really thought they loved each other. I really thought we were a perfect family. I felt so stupid. I was hurt and angry and depressed. I struggled spiritually the whole time. But after about a year, I read through everything I had written in my journal. It kind of hurt to read, but I was absolutely amazed to see how much God was helping me even when I felt all alone. I'm so glad I'll always have those words to turn to when times are tough. I've already decided to share them with a friend who is going through a similar situation in his family.

about getting a letter; one that is written on paper with ink. It comes in a stamped envelope to a metal box sitting on a post in front of your house.

When I go out of town, I call home every night. My wife and kids like that. But they like a card in an envelope underneath their pillow to open and read when they wake up even better.

I've had hundreds and hundreds of great phone conversations with great friends in my life. I have a number of friends with whom I exchange E-mail on a regular basis. But there's something about a card or letter.

Perhaps the number one reason a paper-and-ink letter is better is that it allows us to remember. We forget about phone and E-mail conversations after a little while because they disappear. But letters are there as long as we don't throw them away.

Maybe the most important reason for us to keep a journal of our spiritual walk is that it allows us to remember. Memories are not just lost by the elderly. All of us forget. Through journaling, we preserve our personal spiritual history. We have a record of how God has worked in our lives. Journaling helps us to follow the Old Testament command to remember. We are to remember:

▶ **We were once slaves (Deuteronomy 5:15)—None of us were slaves in Egypt, but all of us were once slaves to sin.**

▶ **The wonders that God has done to deliver us (1 Chronicles 16:12)—When the Israelites looked back at God's wonders, they remembered their exodus from Egypt and all the miracles that God performed to make it happen. For us, we remember the greatest wonder ever performed—Christ's death and resurrection.**

▶ **To proclaim the way that God has worked in our lives (Job 36:24).**

▶ **The gracious deeds of the Lord (Psalm 77:11).**

▶ **God is our Creator (Ecclesiastes 12:1).**

We are called to remember the many ways that the Lord has been a part of our lives. Elie Weisel won a Nobel prize in 1986 for his work and writings on remembering. No, he was not a scientist who researched how we remember and what happens in our brains as we do remember. He was a Jewish scholar who survived Nazi concentration camps during World War II. His life since then has been dedicated to not letting the world forget the brutality and hatred that took place in the camps and in the gas chambers, as over 6 million of his people were exterminated. His reason for remembering was not to heap guilt on any nation. It was so that in remembering, we will never allow an atrocity like the holocaust to happen again in our world.

On a personal level, remembering is not just tied to the past. It is designed so that you grow and become more Christ-like now and in the future. Journaling helps us remember to remember.

What Exactly Is Journaling?

Journaling is like a diary, but it is also very different. When we journal, we write about our past, our present, and our future, so that . . .

1. We better understand ourselves.

You are cherished and valued by God. You have a special place in His heart. Understanding yourself better is an important step in learning to love and cherish yourself the same way God does. It also helps you to face up to your shortcomings and weaknesses and to better recognize your strengths.

2. We deal with emotions like joy, sorrow, anger, and grief in a positive way.

Sometimes it is best to just express your emotions to others as you feel them and get everything out in the open. But sometimes we cannot do that positively. We need time to reflect. We need time to cry or laugh by ourselves. Only then are we ready to share with others what is happening inside of us. I don't want to overly stress keeping a spiritual journal as a psychological cure-all. However, many people have found journaling to be therapeutic and healing.

3. We see God at work in our lives.

If someone were to ask you to explain to him or her how your spiritual life has been progressing lately, it might be hard to pinpoint any details. However, after reading back through your spiritual journal, you might see how you have become more sensitive to the needs of the poor. You might see how your attitude toward your parents has changed for the better. You might see how you forgave a close friend who had hurt you. You might see how God has led you toward full-time Christian service.

Sometimes we have to step back from our immediate situations in order to see how everything is fitting together with God's help.

In many ways your journal will become a record of your

relationship with God. Not everything you write in it will seem religious and spiritual. As you give all of yourself to God, however, you will see that His hand is at work in all of your life. Even the little things—like homework, and the way we interact with little brother or sister—become ways of growing closer to (or more distant from) God. You will be able to note the ups and downs of your relationship with Him. Through this you will learn ways that you can be a more consistent Christian.

4. We enhance our creativity and capture our great ideas.

We often sell ourselves short. It's an easy trap to fall into. If you are not musical or artistic, then obviously you are not creative. Right?

Wrong! Each of us has a creative and imaginative spark inside us that God has planted. It may not show up in how witty we are. We may not win any essay contests. But all of us have unique ideas and ways of looking at life. Such creativity is lost to the church and to others if we don't cultivate it.

5. We reflect on our lifestyle and submit it to the Lord.

Think of some of your friends at school. Why is it that they are getting involved in drug and alcohol abuse? Why are they sexually promiscuous? Why are they constantly apathetic about schoolwork and angry at their parents?

Not only are the teenagers in your school struggling with these and many other issues, but many of them don't even know why. There are reasons; they just aren't evident to that person. The reason they sometimes aren't clear is because we don't encourage reflection in our society.

What we do encourage is:

◗ staying busy every waking hour of the day

◗ watching TV and listening to music until we are numb

◗ being with other people every spare moment we have

Reflection is essential. Not the kind of reflection that turns into self-absorption—thinking about ourselves all the time—but the kind where we positively evaluate our lives: in relation to God, in relation to others, and in relation to ourselves. We ask, "Am I being all that God wants me to be? What needs to change? What needs to stay the same? What needs to improve?"

6. We can express our praise, our thanksgiving, our confession of sins, and our petitions to God.

If this sounds an awful lot like prayer, it's because it is.

Journaling is an excellent way to express your prayers. Not every prayer needs to be written out. But there are times when this is the best way you can express to God what is on your heart.

Get ready to put your spiritual journey in writing—your hopes, your dreams, your prayers, your victories, your failures, your past, and your future. As you do so, a beautiful thing will happen. You will find that God is there to spend time with you, because you have made time for Him.

What Do I Write About?

What you write about in your spiritual journal will most likely fall into two major categories.

▶ Day-by-day accountability

After Jesus sent His 12 disciples into their world to minister in His name, He asked them to report what they had done upon their return. He wanted to know about their successes and failures.

We, too, are sent out by Jesus to minister in His name. And we are accountable for what we have done. We need to ask the question, "How have we been doing, Lord?"

This raises additional questions like: Have we shown God's love to others? Have we followed the leading of the Spirit? Have we obeyed God's commands for our lives? Jesus wants to know.

You understand that this is not for His benefit nearly so much as it is for your benefit. Reporting on your day-to-day activities—the good and the bad—will help you commit all that you do to Jesus' Lordship. It will keep you from going week after week on a downward spiral and then several months down the road wondering—"What happened to my relationship with God?"

This first category deals with the day-to-day, week-to-week routine of your life. You don't write about every detail in your spiritual life, but you will want to choose highlights that characterize the direction your life is going.

▶ Meaningful people, ideas, events, and hopes in my life

Who are the people and what are the events that have influenced my life? What from my past is keeping me from a fruitful walk today? Where am I going? What are my hopes for my future? How can I become a more positive person? How do I deal with my short temper? my too easily hurt feelings? my inability to accept forgiveness?

These are just a few of the questions that you'll deal with

in your journal. Here is where you tie into past, present, and future events and ask the Lord to give you special insight through your thoughts on them.

Two tools are needed for this part of your journaling. The first tool is imagination. We don't usually think of using our imagination as a way of spending time with God. That's too bad, because imagination is one of God's special gifts to us. Through it, He can help us look beyond what we are and picture all that we can be through Him: "Now faith is being sure of what we hope for and certain of what we do not see" (Hebrews 11:1).

The second tool already mentioned a number of times in this chapter is reflection. Too often we go through life—kind of doing well, kind of doing bad; sometimes kind of happy, sometimes kind of sad; sometimes loving others, sometimes rejecting others—without looking beneath the surface, without asking *why*.

Reflection helps us to see what is going on inside of us—to see what is in our hearts. When we examine our hearts through journaling, God will meet us there and confront us with His love and forgiveness and healing and rebuke!

Don't let this sound too heavy or scare you off. Simply begin with the prayer, "Lord, reveal yourself to me in the pages of my life."

Getting Started

What follows are some guidelines and ideas to help you get started with your spiritual journal.

1. Commit your journal to the Lord.

This is the major difference between a spiritual journal and a diary or psychological notebook. We have already noted earlier that one of the major reasons why more people don't spend time with God is that they are too busy. Here you are committing a time of reflection and meditation to God. You are asking Him to help you see yourself and Him more clearly. Each time you write in your journal or breathe a short prayer to God, you are committing your thoughts and words to Him. And as you finish your journal entry, ask the question, "What is God saying to me through what I have written?" Here you can use your imagination and write a short note to yourself from God.

When we commit our journal to the Lord, we avoid the very real danger of being worn down, defeated, and overwhelmed by reflecting on our struggles.

2. Choose your journal.

If you already have a journal, then you're set! If you don't, then take a trip to your local bookstore and browse through the various types of journals on display. Chances are you'll find one just right for you! The most significant differences you'll encounter will have to do with "formatting issues" like size and color. Some journals may include other devotional helps such as motivational quotes or meaningful scriptures along with the journaling space.

There's no right or wrong journal to choose. Your selection should be based on what your unique journaling needs are. Are you wanting to carry your journal around with you? You'll probably want a smaller, more compact journal. Will a quiet and more formal atmosphere help you get into the mood of journaling? If so, then perhaps you'll want to locate a journal that's more "serious" and includes fewer distractions. Do you really like to write, or do you express yourself best in writing? Find a journal that emphasizes the journaling area and includes a lot of journaling pages. There are enough journal options out there that no one should feel forced into using a journal format that isn't right for him or her!

Whatever type of journal you choose, commit to reserving its use *only* for recording your personal journal entries. Don't just use a notebook that is serving another purpose—like keeping notes from your world history class. The reasons are simple. First, it will be harder to keep track of where your different entries are. It is important to review your journal from time to time, and you won't want the pages scattered here and there. Second, it will be more difficult to keep your writings private. You will want to keep your journal in a safe place.

Of course, if you have a computer in your home, you may be more comfortable with an electronic journal. You can purchase a "diary" program in a computer store or catalog, or simply come up with a file name with your regular word processor to save what you write. An electronic journal is often easier to keep safe from prying eyes.

3. Schedule a regular time to journal.

Journaling doesn't happen by accident. You don't just do it when you feel like it. You have to plan for it.

When you first get started, you can plan to write about your spiritual journey once or twice a week. Some people like to write more often than that even in the beginning. You know yourself, so you be the judge of what is a realistic goal for you. Be sure to set a specific time when you will journal. You might want to review your week on Sunday evenings. You might want to commit your week to God on Monday mornings. Set a time and stick with it.

Remember that journaling is a tool to help you spend time with God. It is not a tyrant that controls your life. The goal is to spend time with God, not to write something in your journal every day. Don't neglect journaling or ignore it because "I'm not the sort that writes," but don't let it enslave you either.

4. Keep your journal in a safe place.

Your journal is a personal history. There are times when you will want to share it with others. However, you will write about certain feelings and happenings that are just between you and God. For that reason, do not leave your journal lying around. Be sure that your name, phone number, and address are in the front of it so that if you do leave it somewhere, a person will not have to start rummaging through your entries in order to discover that it is yours.

If you have particularly curious brothers and sisters, you may need to keep it on the top shelf of your closet. This is particularly true if you are working through painful experiences that you don't want anyone else to read right now. When you keep your journal in a safe place, you will feel more free to write about the sensitive issues in your life that God wants to help you work through now.

5. Read through your journal from time to time.

We have already talked about the fact that journaling helps us remember. By looking back through your entries, you will have a tremendous opportunity to note the patterns in your spiritual life.

When were you closest to the Lord? When did you feel yourself drifting? Why were you able to overcome temptation at a certain moment in your life? Why were your attitudes negative toward that friend? How were you able to work through the conflict with your boss?

Reading past entries is not a way to live in the past. It is a reminder of how we are to live at our very best right now!

6. Share your journal with others.

When and if you do share your journal with others is entirely up to you. There will be times when you write about victories in the Lord. You will write about overcoming struggles. You will write about forgiving someone. Let this be your testimony to friends, youth workers, parents, and others who are close to you. There are times when we speak our thoughts on paper more profoundly than we ever could aloud.

This doesn't mean that you have to share everything that you write in your journal. Some people even destroy certain pages after the issue they were dealing with is settled. Why? Because it could become a source of embarrassment to them or others at a later time.

With that warning in mind, remember there are times when you will bless yourself and others by sharing what you have written. One temptation in sharing with others is to explain all that you were feeling and even to apologize for what you have written. No explanation or apologies are necessary. In fact, sharing it will often be more effective if you don't explain or apologize and allow God to use your experience to speak to others as He sees fit.

7. Save your spiritual journal.

Whatever journal format you're using, you will eventually run out of space to journal. Before you rush out to get a new journal, take this opportunity to read through all that you have written. Then, save your writings in a shoe box, a desk drawer, a file folder, or some other stowaway place you devise.

Ten Ideas to Get You Started

Hopefully writing about your daily walk with Christ will come naturally in time. However, many of us need some prompts to help us get started. Here are 10 ideas to get you writing in your own Spending Time with God Journal. By the time you are finished with these 10 ideas, you will have a feel for journaling about the day-to-day events of your spiritual journey, as well as the larger events taking place in your life. Soon you will be coming up with your own ideas and variations of these. Some of these ideas can be repeated over and over.

❶ Write a letter to God. Be very frank. Tell Him exactly where you think you are at this very minute spiritually.

❷ Use your imagination. You are sitting in your bedroom at home. Jesus walks in. What do you say to each other? (Some people ask this question at the end of every journal entry.)

❸ Write the names of five people who have been very special to you in developing your spiritual life. Over the course of several weeks, write a note to each one of them, telling them how much they have meant to you spiritually. (You may want to write this out on another sheet of paper as well and mail it to them.)

❹ Write down the five most discouraging moments you

have had in the past year. Then write out a speech and tell "Discouragement" why you aren't going to let it ruin your life—or even one year.

5 Think back to a happy moment when you were around five years old. Describe your feelings as best you remember them. Then write a prayer to God, asking Him to help you have the faith of a child.

6 Write down the names of six or seven superstars that your friends at school admire. Choose one of them, and write out what you would like to say to him or her about the spiritual impact—positive or negative—he or she has on your friends' lives and on your life.

7 Write down the characteristics you would like to find in a husband or wife. Using your imagination, describe a little about this person's life. Now, write a letter to yourself, asking the questions: "Do your dating habits honor the person you want to marry someday? Are you growing in the characteristics someone else will want in a spouse?"

8 Write down five goals you have for your life by the time you are age 20, and then five more that you want to reach by age 30. Choose one that you want to reach by age 20. Write out what you will have to do to achieve this goal, beginning today. Later on you can select other goals about which to write.

9 Think of the last time you experienced any emotion very strongly—anger, sorrow, fear, or joy. Why did you experience the emotion? What lesson can you learn from it? How does God help you work through negative emotions?

10 Put yourself in your parents' shoes. Think like them for just a minute. Now write a "parental talk" to yourself from them. Here are a few of the things you can write about: My greatest hope for you is . . . ; My greatest fear for you is . . . ; I am proud of you because . . . ; The most important thing you can learn from me is . . .

These are just a few ideas to get you going. You will think of others. Remember, commit your journaling to the Lord. Let Him speak to you as you reflect on your life.

Your Reactions and Actions

1. Your imagination can have a positive or negative impact on your spiritual life. Write down one way it can be positive and one way it could be negative.

2. When does reflection become unhealthy for your spiritual life?

3. When it comes to remembering God's gracious deeds in your life, how do you rate?

├──────────────┼──────────────┼──────────────┤
I remember well   *I forget too easily*

4. Write down three of your own ideas you can use in your spiritual journal.

5. Why not begin journaling now? Start by writing a short paragraph describing what your spiritual journey has been like in the last couple of days ("Day-by-day accountability"). Then look back at the 10 journaling ideas mentioned above ("Meaningful people, ideas, events, and hopes in my life"). Choose one and write another short paragraph. (Don't forget to commit this time to God!)

...Through Prayer

**I have been driven many times to my knees by the
overwhelming conviction that I had nowhere else to go.
My own wisdom, and that of all about me,
seemed insufficient for the day.**
—Abraham Lincoln

Devote yourselves to prayer, being watchful and thankful.
(Colossians 4:2)

Tony and Angela and Prayer

"Did you do OK on your test, Tony?"

"I don't think so, Angela."

"What happened?"

"Well, I really didn't study enough. The Bears were on *Monday Night Football* and all."

"Naturally. So you watched the game instead of studying."

"Right. What'd you think I'd do? I did try to cover my bases, though."

"I thought bases were with baseball."

"Very funny, Angela. I see that my sense of humor is finally rubbing off on you."

"That's kind of scary."

"I'll ignore that last remark. What I did was follow the advice of Pastor Hensley. I kind of thought

Bruce:
I admit that my prayer life isn't as good as it should be. I struggle to concentrate. My mind skips to other things. One minute I'm praying for a friend at school, the next minute I'm thinking of the football game on Friday night. A bunch of us in my youth group were praying for a friend who is real sick. I felt bad because all I could think about the whole time was asking this girl in the group out for a date. My dad told me not to worry about it—he has the same problem. But I really do want to have the kind of prayer life I hear about from others. I do love God. I just don't seem to pray very well. My English teacher has us write in a journal every day at school. I'm going to try writing out my prayers in her class.

that praying might help. So I prayed that God would help me on the test. But I don't think God answered this one."

"Imagine that."

"What's with the sarcasm? You don't think God should answer my prayers. It says right in the Bible we should ask for whatever we want. Right?"

"Yes, Tony, it does. But—"

"That settles it then. It says it in the Bible, and I believe the Bible. Besides, that's what Pastor Hensley said on Sunday too."

"I don't think you heard his whole sermon, Tony."

"I know I missed part of it while I was reading my Sunday School paper, but other than that I listened pretty well last week."

"Tony!"

"Yes, Angela?"

"Has anyone told you that you are exasperating?"

"My mother has many times. But I didn't know what it meant when she said it either."

"That doesn't surprise me."

"You're just changing the subject because you know I'm right. We can ask God for anything, because we are His children. He likes to give good gifts to His children, as the pastor said."

"I believe that, Tony. I just have one question. Why didn't God answer your prayer, then?"

"Uh . . ."

"Yes?"

"Uh, well, I hadn't really thought of that. Maybe I don't have enough faith."

"That could be. But maybe there is more to prayer than late-night pleas for help for a test you didn't study for."

"Hey, it wasn't a late-night plea for help. I prayed for help that very morning!"

"Yes, Tony, you really are exasperating."

"Thanks, Angela! I'll take that as a compliment."

What Is Prayer?

Tony is not all wrong about prayer. We are told that if we have faith and do not doubt, we can move mountains and will receive whatever we ask for in prayer (Matthew 21:21-22). However, Tony really did miss out on a good part of the sermon and a lot of other truths we need to know about prayer.

Tony reflects a tendency we have to limit our talk about

prayer. We do this through focusing on several questions over and over:

Why doesn't God answer all *of my prayers?*

If God knows everything, then why do I even have to ask Him for anything?

Since God knows best, why would He listen to my prayers?

These are important questions. But they only deal with one aspect of prayer: our requests. What we need to discover is that prayer is much more than simply asking God for things.

The very simplest way to understand prayer is to realize that it is conversation with God. At the heart of prayer is a dialogue with the Creator of the universe. How many of us have conversations with friends that are always one-sided—"Will you do this or that for me?"—without feeling that something is wrong with the relationship? Such "dialogue" gets old very quickly.

Prayer is not to be a one-way process where we bring our list of requests to God and hope that He answers them. There are at least four other elements of prayer that we need to know about and make a part of our lives, as well as some reminders that we need to take to heart, if our conversation with God is to be all it can be.

Before we look at the five major elements of prayer, here are the reminders to take to heart:

1. Prayer is God's gracious invitation to you.

It wasn't exactly a swearword. But for a third grader, what I had called the young lady sitting next to me on the bus returning to school from a field trip was totally unacceptable. When the call came to our classroom, and I received an invitation from the principal to visit with him, I knew I was in trouble—big trouble. As I trudged toward his office, the halls seemed higher, narrower, longer, and darker than they ever had before. Those were the pre-student-liberation days when principals could still wash students' mouths out with soap. I remember quite clearly that he did exactly that.

In contrast to this bleak picture, we read in Hebrews, "Therefore, brothers, since we have confidence to enter the Most Holy Place by the blood of Jesus, by a new and living way opened for us through the curtain, that is, his body, and since we have a great priest over the house of God, let us draw near to God with a sincere heart" (10:19-22).

Mark it on your calendar. You have been invited into the

presence of God Almighty. Through Jesus Christ, our Great High Priest, you can confidently draw near to God. Take advantage of this gracious privilege.

2. Prayer begins with listening.

We have already noted that prayer is not simply one-way communication. Too often, though, we reduce prayer to a time when we present God with a list of what we want and need help on.

God, I need help with my parents. Would You help them be more understanding?

God, it seems as if I never get a break. Would You help me get a starting position on the football team this year?

God, I don't know where to go to college. Would You send me a message?

There is nothing wrong with bringing petitions to God. We are encouraged to do so. However, do you take the time to pause and listen for God's voice? Do you quiet your heart before Him and say, "Lord, I want to hear Your voice today"?

3. Prayer is empowered through faith.

Here is that reminder about faith again. There are no magic formulas, special rites, incantations, concentration drills, or anything else that will help you spend time with God through prayer—without faith. For prayer to be effective, it must come from a trust and strong belief in God's love for you and His willingness to act in your life.

4. Prayer is learned.

In Luke 11:1, we read that Jesus took His disciples away from the crowds in order to teach them to pray. As with other methods of spending time with God, prayer, too, takes learning.

What this means is that prayer will not always come naturally for you. You will have to practice and grow in your praying skills. If you doubt this in any way, take a break right now to quiet yourself and to listen for God's voice. Spend just 30 seconds doing this. This could very well feel strange, awkward, and unproductive for you. Why? Because the muscles of your prayer life need to develop and be toned.

You may not see any immediate results from your prayers as you get started. You may not sense God's presence. But as you develop your prayer life, you will find that prayer is a great source of power, freedom, and guidance in your life.

Five Dynamics of Prayer

1. Praise

You know how great you feel when someone praises you. A coach, a teacher at school, a music instructor, your parents, or someone else important to you says, "Good job!" You feel great because someone has spoken well of you. That is what praise is: speaking well of someone.

When we praise God, we speak well of Him. We recognize that He:

◗ created the universe and every living thing in it—including you

◗ redeemed us through the blood of Jesus, who died on the Cross and rose again for our sins

◗ has never forsaken His promise to love and care for us

God is all-powerful, all-knowing, good, faithful, and loving. It is no wonder that God wants us to praise Him. Certainly praise brings pleasure to God. But more than that, praise is good for us. It serves as a constant reminder to us of who God is and who we are. He is the Creator. We are created. Praise is our way of remembering that we are not independent agents. We are dependent on God's continued activity and interest in our lives and in our world. Even if we and everybody else fails to take time to praise God for who He is, the fact remains that we are dependent upon Him.

In Romans 1:21-23, we read: "For although they knew God, they neither glorified him as God nor gave thanks to him, but their thinking became futile and their foolish hearts were darkened. Although they claimed to be wise, they became fools and exchanged the glory of the immortal God for images made to look like mortal man and birds and animals and reptiles."

In our culture, the worship of "images" is alive and well. These idols are not necessarily made of stone, gold, or silver. But the idols of scientific accomplishment, human understanding, and material possessions can be seen everywhere.

Foolish people continue to worship the created rather than the Creator. When we take time to praise God in our prayer life, we are able to avoid the devastating sin of pride.

Take a rest from reading right now, and write out a short prayer of praise to God in the space on the next page. Use your journal to write out a note of praise to God each day.

My Praise to God

2. Thanksgiving

For many, thanksgiving really does come only once a year—oh, and of course, three times a day at mealtime (twice if you don't bow your head in the school cafeteria).

We don't live in an overly thankful world. And I must admit, I often don't remember to be grateful for all I have and have been given. Oh, all of us give thanks for the obvious acts of kindness—

I appreciate the sweater you got me for Christmas, Grandma.

Thanks for helping me with my homework, Dave.

Wow! I can't believe you got me the new CD I wanted, Mom.

But overall, most of us aren't as grateful as we should be. We emphasize what we don't get rather than what we have been given.

How often do you thank your parents for what they have done for you? Or, like so many others, do you usually complain about what they haven't done?

The second attitude of prayer is thanksgiving. In Psalm 105, we are instructed to approach God with an attitude of thanksgiving, praising Him and remembering everything He has done on our behalf. In Philippians 4:4-8, we are told to give thanks in all things. We thank God for all that we have and all that He has done for us. We acknowledge that every gift and talent we possess is from God.

Do we thank God even when bad things happen? Do we even thank God for the things about us that we don't like?

According to Philippians 4:6, we are to give thanks in all situations: "In *everything,* by prayer and petition, *with thanksgiving,* present your requests to God" (emphasis added).

This doesn't mean we are thankful that bad things have happened. We are thankful *in spite of* them. We focus on the half-full glass, instead of always noting the half that's empty. We don't blissfully ignore the bad. But even in the worst of situations, we can at least be thankful that God is with us and will never forsake us!

The attitude of thankfulness is of course closely related to praise. The difference is that we praise God for who He is. We thank God for what He has done for us and the many gifts and talents He has given to us.

Why not begin now to cultivate the attitude of thanksgiving. List at least a couple of things you have to be thankful for in each of the following three areas.

At Home	At School	At Church

If you find that creating this list requires quite a bit of work, realize that this is a particular phrase of prayer you will really need to develop. Now write down a brief prayer on thanksgiving in the space below. Remember this important aspect of your prayer life as you use your journal each day.

My Thanksgiving to God

3. Confession

Perhaps the hardest thing to do inside the church or outside the church is to admit failure.

I was wrong. I blew it. I messed up. I sinned.

I remember sometime during my fifth or sixth grade year going over to the corner drugstore with a friend. You already know where this story is going, don't you? There we committed two of the vilest of childhood sins. We stole. And not only did we steal, but we stole cigarettes.

After smoking a pack of cigarettes down by the creek and turning a mild shade of green, I returned home that night feeling very guilty and more than a little bit sick. I had a hard time looking anyone in the eyes. I didn't feel right. It seemed that everyone was looking at me. I knew I had done wrong.

I went to bed, but I couldn't sleep. So late into the night—it must have been all of 10:30—I padded downstairs and told my parents what I had done. The next day my dad took me over to the store, and we paid for the pack of cigarettes.

What a painful and humiliating experience. That's what makes confession so hard. Imagine the humiliation that David experienced when he confessed to his adulterous affair with Bathsheba and the way he had her husband killed to cover it up. In Psalm 51, David cried out in real agony as he acknowledged that he had sinned against God and man.

When face-to-face with the realization of his sinfulness, Isaiah falls to his face and cries, "Woe is me!" (6:5, KJV).

It is not very precise theologically, but one of the ways that I view confession is this: Anything that hurts that much must be good for you! It is kind of like the brussels sprouts of your prayer life.

I believe that the current emphasis in our culture on "feeling good about myself" is positive when it comes to recognizing that God has created us with infinite worth. We can love and accept ourselves because God loves and accepts us just as we are. However, this does not give us the green light to passively accept sinning and doing wrong—and to feel good about it. God's love is no salve to ease our conscience when we do so. God does love the sinner, but He continues to hate sin. Confession opens us to the cleansing power of Jesus' blood (1 John 1:7).

Confession is not just good for the soul. Confession is essential to maintaining a relationship with God. It cannot be left out of our prayer life. With David, we acknowledge any sin against God and others. We ask for forgiveness. In doing so, we acknowledge the seriousness of sin. We are chastened. We are motivated not to sin anymore. We are cleansed, so that we can continue our fellowship with God.

Have you had a time in your life like David? Do you have any unresolved sin in your life? Are there some ways that you are falling short of all that God wants you to be? Why don't you acknowledge this simply and briefly right now.

My Confession to God

4. Petitions

We are told to take everything to God in prayer, including our needs and wants. Keep in mind:

- ◐ God desires that we bring our requests to Him. James says, "You do not have, because you do not ask God" (4:2). Just as parents desire to know their child's needs, so God wants us to bring our needs before Him.

- ◐ Our ultimate prayer is like that of Jesus in the garden: "Not my will, but thine" (Luke 22:42, KJV). This reminder serves as a major deterrent to praying selfishly and from wrong motives. It is again James who tells us, "When you ask, you do not receive, because you ask with wrong motives" (4:3). When we tell God, "Not my will, but Your will, be done," we will keep our motives on track.

- ◐ Sometimes God answers, "No." I would like to give my children everything they desire. However, I would not be a responsible parent if I were to do so. Some things are harmful for them; other things they aren't ready for. For that reason, God sometimes does not grant our requests. As you bring your requests to God, keep in mind that He sees more than you do. Be willing to withdraw and change your requests as you sense God saying no to what you have brought before Him.

- ◐ Sometimes God answers in a manner different than we expect. We ask God to change our parents so that family life will be better. He might point out instead that the change must start with you to make family life better. Part of having faith is having a confident expectancy. That's great. However, don't let this expectancy turn into inflexible expectations of just how God is to answer your prayers. He probably has a better way to answer your prayer than you could ever think of!

- ◐ Sometimes we have to wait for answers. We definitely live in a NOW society. Fast-food restaurants ensure that you have your food now. Once you are out on your own and making money, credit card companies will work with you so that you can have any gadget or gizmo you want right now—whether or not you can afford it.

Keep in mind that sometimes you will have to wait for answers to your prayers. It's a great idea to begin praying today for the person you will marry sometime in the future. However, if you are 16 right now, don't expect to meet him or her within the next few weeks (or years!).

With all that is being said so far, it might seem as though I'm trying to explain things away so that you won't be disappointed or lose faith when your prayers are not answered. I don't believe so. In my own life and in the lives of people close to me, I have seen answers to specific requests. Read on!

- ❍ Your needs will be met. Jesus reminds His disciples in the Sermon on the Mount that there is no need to worry about the basic needs of life: "Look at the birds of the air; they do not sow or reap or store away in barns, and yet your heavenly Father feeds them. Are you not much more valuable than they?" (Matthew 6:26). This is no call to irresponsibility. It is a reminder of God's continued concern for our lives. He knows our needs and will supply them.

- ❍ Don't be surprised when God does answer your prayers! Have you ever prayed for something, seen it happen, and then not given God the credit? "Maybe it was a coincidence!" One person has noted that "coincidences" always occurred much more often in his life when he prayed than when he didn't pray. Don't be surprised by some "coincidences" in your life that look like answers to prayer.

- ❍ Don't forget to thank God for answers to your prayers. You may need to reread the "Thanksgiving" section of this chapter several more times before you get the hang of it. I know I constantly need to remind myself to thank God for what He is doing in my life. In Luke 17:11-19, 10 lepers were healed by Jesus. How many remembered to give Him thanks? Only one. You may be in the minority, but it seems only right to be a person who remembers to say, "Thanks, Jesus."

Are there needs in your life right now? Why don't you write them down on the left side of the chart below. Come back to the book and, as answers are received, record them.

My Petitions to God

Requests   *Answers*

5. Intercession

There is a special kind of prayer called "intercession." What happens in intercessory prayer is that we go before God on behalf of someone else. Often, intercession is for someone who is not a Christian and who will not pray for himself or herself.

This is what makes intercessory prayer so hard to understand. We know that everyone is responsible for his or her own life before God. No one can force someone else to become a Christian, and God will not force anyone to do so, either. However, when we intercede in prayer for someone else, a special conviction and awareness of God can take place in that person's life. The Holy Spirit will communicate to that person in a more intense way just because we prayed. The major factor is not his or her faithfulness but your, the intercessor's, faithfulness.

We can also intercede for people when:

—they are ill,

—they are facing trials and tribulations,

—they are going through any situation where they need the extra support of other Christians.

Intercession is, for many, a powerful ministry. But it is not easy. It takes steadfast persistence, stretching faith, tears and deep feelings for the person, and often fasting and the help of others uniting with you in prayer.

We can't forget, particularly when we are praying for someone's salvation, that God will not violate that person's free will. He has given everyone the choice to live for or against Him. What you can do is bombard them in such a way that they are keenly aware of God's presence. The person alone determines how he or she will respond to such an awareness of God.

I'm grateful for the prayers that others have offered on my behalf. I am sure there were some times when special protection was granted to me because of them. I also know that there are some others for whom I want to continue to pray: that they will find God; that they will stand strong when they face temptation; that they will sense God's comfort in a special way.

Is there someone for whom you want to pray? Someone for whom you are carrying a particular burden? Write down his or her name. Perhaps you are ready to take on the ministry of intercession.

Pray Without Ceasing

Prayer is not just for alone times. Prayer needs to be a habit that is cultivated as an ongoing process and force in your life. Don't just pray in the morning for Scott. Pray for him silently as you pass him in the hall at school. Don't just pray during family devotions that things will go better for your mom at work, but pray for her when you see the teacher who looks a little bit like her.

Put reminders for yourself in your books, in your pockets, on your clothing, in your room, so that prayer will be a conversation with God throughout your day. Get in the habit of offering short prayers to Him all day long.

Your Attitude in Prayer

Proper reverence for God is always a must. The first four of the Ten Commandments give us guidance for the proper honor and respect we are to show to our Heavenly Father. For example, we are not to take God's name in vain—that is, use it lightly.

But we should also note that in Romans 8:15, Paul tells us that we can call on God as *"Abba,* Father." *Abba* simply means "Daddy." God is not some distant ruler who wishes us to grovel before Him. He is a loving "Daddy."

You can come to God in prayer with the same familiarity as if you were going to an earthly father who was very gentle and loving. You do not have to pray in Elizabethan English. You can talk to Him in the same way you would talk to your best friend, using the same type of words and voice. This is not a sign of disrespect, but it is our way of accepting God's invitation to be a part of His immediate family.

Prayer and Fasting

Fasting is a voluntary self-denial of food and sometimes (though not usually) of liquids. The purpose of fasting is to give up food for a period of time in order to devote special attention to our spiritual life and other spiritual issues. Perhaps there is a nagging problem in your life. Perhaps you need God's guidance on a particular issue. Perhaps you keenly feel the need to pray for your parents. Perhaps you and some other friends from your youth group want to lift before God in a united way a teen who is straying. Fasting will help you focus on the spiritual help that is needed.

Some Christians regularly fast. They are following both Old and New Testament witnesses of its importance. Others never fast. In Matthew 6:16, Jesus warns that fasting must be done with the right motives—not for the attention and admiration of others. However, Jesus does seem to think that fasting is a normal practice for His followers because He says, "*When* you fast" (emphasis added). The important issue to keep in mind is that fasting is to be done for a spiritual reason.

From a physical standpoint, don't try too much (or is that *too little?*) when you first fast. A 24-hour period may be too much for you the first several times you fast. Try fasting for one or two meals at first. Be sure to drink plenty of fluids— many recommend only water. Be sure to accompany your fast with prayer. And do not worry about a growling stomach. Believe it or not, you probably won't ever experience real hunger the first day of any fast. That is only the sound of a pampered tummy.

Journaling and Prayer

Like reading the Bible, prayer is not optional. Prayer does need to be a part of our daily life. You don't *have* to write in a journal every day to have an effective prayer life. However, journaling can be a useful tool in developing this important element of your spiritual life.

Why write out prayers? By following the outline mentioned earlier, and by writing several sentences for each section, you will help yourself focus more on the different dynamics of prayer. And you may find it easier to express in written words all that you want to communicate to God.

Your Reactions and Actions

1. How would you rate your prayer life at this point in time? Is it . . .

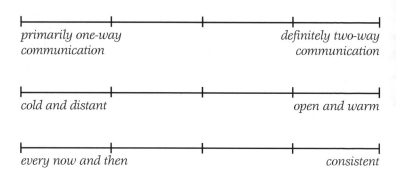

primarily one-way
communication

definitely two-way
communication

cold and distant

open and warm

every now and then

consistent

2. In which area of prayer do you need to grow the most? Circle it.

Praise   Thanksgiving   Confession   Petition   Intercession

What do you plan to do about it?

3. Can you think of something besides food—like TV or radio—that might be good for you to "fast" for 24 hours or more?

4. Read Matthew 26:39-42, Jesus' prayer at Gethsemane. Is there a particular area in your life where you are struggling to say, "'Yet not as I will, but as you will,' Lord"?

STWG...

5

. . . Through Time in His Word

The longer you read the Bible, the more you will like it; it will grow sweeter and sweeter; and the more you get into the spirit of it, the more you will get into the Spirit of Christ.

—Romaine

▰▰▰▰

How can a young man keep his way pure? By living according to your word. I seek you with all my heart; do not let me stray from your commands. I have hidden your word in my heart that I might not sin against you.

(Psalm 119:9-11)

Underline These Words!

I leaned forward as the evangelist said . . .

Before you leave this camp, I want you to underline Philippians chapter 4, verses 4 through 8. In fact, if you have your Bible and a pen or pencil with you, I want you to do it right now.

Since I had my Bible and pen on hand, I underlined those verses as he continued:

There is a good reason that I want you to do this, teens. And I want you to listen to me very carefully so you don't miss it. You are going to leave this camp tomor-

Ashley:

I asked my parents for a new Bible, so they got me one for my birthday. It slips into a neat leather cover that they bought for me too. The great thing is that the words are pretty easy to understand. I used to have problems following it all the time. Now I know what the Bible means. Plus there are articles and questions and devotions to help me apply the Bible to my everyday life. I'm not sure I am what you would call a great Bible student. But I do read from God's Word every day, and I find it helps me in every area of my life. Thanks, Mom and Dad. This might be the best gift you ever gave me!

47

*row. You will probably forget most of what I have said. The emo-
tional high that you are feeling now is going to go away. You are
going to face temptations. You are going to feel discouraged at
times. And yes, you are going to fail at times.*

*The reason I want you to underline Philippians chapter 4,
verses 4 through 8, and the reason I want you to start underlining
verses in your Bible is so that when you do leave camp, and your
emotions go from sky-high to way low, and when you face temptations, and get discouraged, and yes, even when you fail—you
won't lose what you got this week. Like nothing else, God's Word
will keep you going in your Christian walk.*

I was 17 years old when I heard those words. I was at teen
camp, two weeks before my senior year of high school. I had
made a commitment to follow Jesus Christ during the Tues-
day morning chapel service that week.

Sure enough, the evangelist was right. I went home, and
the very next day I did experience an emotional letdown. I
looked temptation right in the face. At times it seemed to be
my constant companion. Over and over I prayed, "Lord, does
it get any easier?"

I experienced discouragement. And yes, I failed. I fell on
my face more times than I like to remember.

However, I had underlined Philippians 4:4-8, just as the
evangelist suggested. They were the very first verses that I
had marked in my brand-new Bible. I began underlining other
passages—like 1 John 1:7; Romans 12:1-2; Hebrews 12:1-4; 1
Timothy 4:12; James 1:12; and many others.

Sometimes joyfully, sometimes out of duty, and sometimes not quite all the way into it, I worked at making the
Bible a part of my life. And sure enough, that evangelist was
right again. Spending time with God through His Word kept
me on the Christian journey. Yes, there were times I asked for
forgiveness of sins—often it was the Word that reminded me
of this need. And, yes, there were dry spells.

Yet since that camp, I have striven to be a Christian and all
that God has wanted me to be. I believe that in spite of my
stubbornness, my weaknesses, my pride, and the different
temptations that have come my way, I have remained a Christian because of God's Word.

In your desire to live the Christian life, you *must* spend
time with God in His Word, the Bible. It is not optional. It is
not a when-I-feel-like-it type thing. It is a habit you must cultivate. There are several good reasons.

The Benefits of Spending Time in God's Word

Good things happen in your life when you start spending time with God through His Word. Reading your Bible daily will . . .

▶ Help you become established in your spiritual journey

David said that whoever delights and "meditates" on "the law of the LORD . . . is like a tree planted by streams of water" (Psalm 1:2-3). For David, and the people of his day, the "law" referred to the first five books of the Old Testament, the Torah. We have found this same truth to apply to all of our Scriptures, both Old and New Testaments.

By making God's Word a vital part of your life, you, too, will be well nourished, deep-rooted, and fruitful in your spiritual life.

▶ Help you overcome temptation

"I have hidden your word in my heart that I might not sin against you" was David's prayer of praise to God in Psalm 119:11. By making God's Word a vital part of our lives, we, too, can join David in this song. We live in days that are dangerous to our spiritual health. Both subtle and obvious sins are everywhere. You jeopardize your spiritual walk if you don't arm yourself with God's Word to face temptation. There are no exceptions. This is true for everyone.

Brian, a junior in high school, was out with a group of his friends one Friday night. A couple of the guys had fake IDs. They wanted to sneak everyone into a bar just for the fun of it. Brian turned them down and had the driver drop him off at home. Later that night, two of his friends were beat up in a fight.

"I might have been with them," Brian said, "except I remembered part of that verse in Romans, 'Do not be conformed . . . , but be transformed' [12:2, NKJV]. I knew it was important for me to stand up and be counted."

▶ Help you know God's will

In Psalm 119:105, David says that God's Word "is a lamp to [his] feet and a light for [his] path." People are looking every which way for direction in life. There are self-help books by the thousands, and cults and other new religions are springing up everywhere to show people "the way."

You have questions about your present and future. What will I do for a living? Whom will I marry? What college, if any, should I go to? How can I get along with my parents and brothers and sisters?

You need to realize that all the principles for you to have a meaningful life are found in the Bible. No other source has proved trustworthy like God's Word. Many errors arise from ignoring this Source of direction for right living. God's Word will keep you on track!

▶ Bring joy into your life

Again looking at Psalm 119, this time at verse 103, David says that God's Word is like "honey to [his] mouth." Rather than bringing one more tedious job and responsibility into your life, making the Bible a part of your life will be a great source of joy and pleasure. Of course it will be hard work at times. There will be days when there doesn't seem to be a message just for you. But the effort you make will have its rewards as you spend time with, and become a better friend with, the true Source of joy, Jesus Christ, and as you let the Bible impact your life.

"I've Tried This Before, You Know, and . . ."

So you've tried starting a regular time of personal Bible study before. Don't tell me. It didn't seem to work.

How'd you know?

Let's just say, you're not alone. Many people have resolved to make the Bible a vital part of their lives, only to fail. Right now, at this very moment in your life as you read these words, it is not as important that you have failed in the past as it is that you are willing to try again.

There are thousands and thousands of other teenagers your age with schedules, with teachers, with homework, with commitments, with distractions, with study habits, with reading skills, and with a bunch of other things just like yours, who have made the Bible a part of their lives. You can too. Remember what was said earlier: Set reasonable goals for yourself. You probably won't be able to read through the entire Bible this year. You may not even be able to read through the New Testament this year! You may start out by only studying five or six verses a day. What counts right now is for you to get started, spending some time in the Word every day.

Here are some guidelines to help make Bible reading and study a dynamic, I-can-hardly-wait-for-what-God's-got-for-me-today experience.

How to Read and Study the Bible

1. Have your own Bible.

Having your own Bible—not one that is sitting on your

shelf collecting dust, not one that your Sunday School teacher passes out to you each week—is the place to start. Your own Bible is the one that has your name in it. The one that is written in a way that you can understand it. The one that you not only carry to Sunday School but even remember to bring home with you. And yes (get ready for this), the Bible you even carry to school with you (without a civics textbook cover wrapped around it). You need a Bible that you cherish and keep close at hand.

2. Begin with prayer.

Every time you sit down to read your Bible, ask God to speak to you through the portion of Scripture you will be studying that day. Let Him know you are ready and willing to hear His voice. Let Him know that you want to obey what His Word has to say to you. Let God know that you desire to spend time with Him.

3. Plan a Bible-reading schedule.

Hit-and-miss jumps into Scripture can be fruitful. There are instances when a person has been absolutely in the dumps, only to open to a page of Scripture and—voilà—have just the right message from God jump out at him or her. However, you may profit more on a day-to-day basis if you read entire books of the Bible at a time, not just parts here and there.

As you map out a Bible-reading schedule, you will want to start by reading books of the Bible that are easier to understand. All Scripture is given by God for our good. I'm not suggesting that you ignore certain portions, but some scripture is harder to understand and may not apply as directly to your life right now. Save that scripture for when you are a more mature Bible student.

If you don't already have a place to start in your Bible study, here are some suggested books of the Bible you may want to read first.

- ◐ James
- ◐ The Gospel of Mark
- ◐ 1 John
- ◐ Psalms—try the first 23, then move on to another section of the Bible
- ◐ The Gospel of John
- ◐ Proverbs
- ◐ Acts
- ◐ Genesis
- ◐ 1 and 2 Timothy

4. Use a study method.

You have plenty of studying to do at school. Study in and of itself doesn't sound very appealing. However, part of being a disciple is having discipline. Discipline leads to growth and maturity. It does not even have to be a bad or negative word. Athletics and many other pursuits illustrate that discipline leads to positive and healthy experiences in our lives.

As you read on and learn one simple Bible study method, you are going to see how writing your Bible study in a spiritual journal can be used to make your time in the Word more effective.

STEP ONE
Look for the Big Picture

Before focusing on several verses or a particular chapter, get an overall idea of the type of book you are reading. Try to find out who is writing the book, to whom it is being written, and why it is being written. Many Bibles contain a short introduction to each of the books of the Bible with a lot of this information provided.

Another way to do this is to read the entire book quickly. *(What?!)* Don't panic. I did use the word *quickly.*

But I'm a slow reader. This will take me forever.

If it is a longer book of the Bible, simply skim through all of it, and note the paragraph headings that are printed in your Bible. Remember, this first step is not the Bible study itself. You are not trying to read every word. You are getting acquainted with the flow, the mood, and the feeling of the book.

STEP TWO
Select a Study Passage

Once you have an idea of the big picture, you will want to start studying at chapter 1, verse 1 of the book you are reading. It is not required that you study every verse in the book that you are reading, but you will want to at least read every verse once. Select anywhere from three or four verses to an entire chapter on which to concentrate each day.

When you were looking for the big picture, you were trying to skim as many verses as you could. When you *study* a passage, what counts is your quality of reading, not your quantity of reading. One caution: Try not to break up paragraphs, or you may lose the meaning of the passage as a whole.

STEP THREE
Read the Study Passage Several Times

After you choose the verses you're going to study, read that section of Scripture at least two times. Three or four times would be better. You will not be able to understand the scripture or have exciting insights into it until you know what it says. One way this is done is through repetition. Again, if you are worried that you are too slow a reader to be able to do all this, remember that you set the pace. You can choose to study a chapter or just a few verses. What counts is that you grow in an understanding of God's Word.

STEP FOUR
Search for Major Truths

As you read through your study passage for the third or fourth time, note the key thoughts found there. What is the writer trying to get across? What does he want the people who read this to understand? What is his major point or points?

Search for:

- Commands to be obeyed
- Warnings to be heeded
- Promises to be claimed
- Truths to be believed

Begin to jot down these key thoughts and major truths in your Spending Time with God Journal or another notebook. Write in a way that you can remember what you read. This is not necessarily for English class, so you do not have to use complete sentences (unless that's how you'll remember best!). You might even simply write key words. Note the style used in the sample journal entry at the end of this chapter.

STEP FIVE
Ask Questions—and Look for Answers

Now is the time to raise questions or note the questions that have already come to your mind. Not everything in the Bible is immediately or easily understood. Don't be surprised or intimidated or frustrated by this fact. It was the apostle Peter who said of Paul's writings: "His letters contain some things that are hard to understand" (2 Peter 3:16).

Use your journal to record questions you have about the scripture you are reading. What doesn't make sense? What don't you understand? Of course, you won't be satisfied to simply write down your questions. Here are several places where you can go to get answers to these questions.

◐ Scripture

Other verses of Scripture will help answer your questions. Sometimes it is best to let the Bible explain itself. If you have a study Bible, next to the verse you are studying you will see a list of scriptures that deal with the same theme. Look these verses up, and see if they shed light on your verse.

In the back of your Bible, or as a separate book in your church's library, there is also a concordance. A concordance is an alphabetical listing of major biblical words, with a list of the Bible verses where these words are used. This can help you understand a particular word by the way it is used in other passages.

◐ Commentaries

You can also find answers to your questions in Bible commentaries. Commentaries study and explain the Bible, moving from verse to verse, or sometimes paragraph to paragraph. Commentaries are also a good place to help you get a big picture of the scripture you are studying. Your church library probably contains several sets of commentaries you could borrow.

◐ Pastors and teachers

Your pastor and Sunday School teachers are also good resources. It may come as a shock to you, but your parents might also be excellent resource people to go to with some questions. Any of these human sources may not be able to give you an answer right away—don't let that surprise you. But they will be willing to search for answers with you.

Many of these resources are conveniently packaged for you in youth study Bibles and software packages.

STEP SIX
Put It into Practice

You need to apply the Bible to your life now. "Do not merely listen to the word . . . *Do what it says*" (1:22, emphasis added) was James's advice in his letter to Christians scattered everywhere. He goes on to say that if you listen to the Word but fail to practice it, you are like a person who looks in the mirror and then turns away and forgets what he or she looks like (vv. 23-24).

Is there something you are doing that you shouldn't be doing? Or, is there something you are not doing that you need to be doing? Is there something about God or Jesus or the Holy Spirit that you did not know before? Do you need to be more sensitive to someone at school? Do you need to seek someone's forgiveness? Do you need to forgive someone?

Jot these things down. Again, how you write it is not as important as the fact that you are writing it down in a way that you can remember. Remembering does not ensure that you will act on these truths. But trying to remember is an excellent place to start. It draws your attention to what is right and best for your life.

STEP SEVEN
Select a Verse to Memorize

The final step in your Bible study is to take one last look at your study passage and write down a verse or two that you want to remember most. Memorizing scripture is a terrific discipline. It allows you to take scripture with you, even when you don't or can't have your Bible at hand. In our country, with its millions upon millions of Bibles, we are not as appreciative of this point as we should be. However, all of us have been in situations and faced temptations when we needed to have a verse of Scripture at hand.

Writing out a key verse will make remembering it much easier for you. It's also a great way to make memorizing a verse a lot easier.

Jump In! The Water Feels Great!

As we have worked through this simple, yet powerful, Bible study method, have you made the decision to get to know God's Word and make it a vital part of your life? Are you ready to get started today? There really is no better time to begin than the next 10 or 20 minutes. If you already have a journal, why not put this book to the side and use your journal now? Or take a blank sheet of paper and follow the seven-step outline you just learned.

A good book of the Bible for you to get started in is James. Why don't you study the first 12 verses? Don't forget the big picture. First, try to skim the entire book quickly (there are only five chapters). From there, look forward to claiming some exciting promises that God has for you in His Word.

Your Reactions and Actions

1. In your own words, why is studying the Word so important to spending time with God?

2. Can you remember a time when a portion of God's Word was especially helpful to you?

3. Without looking back in the chapter, can you remember the seven steps for studying the Bible?

4. Why don't you take on a little project! Call your pastor to set up a time for him or her to show you around your church's library and possibly even his or her personal library. Ask about some of the commentaries and Bible study aids found there. You might ask which books help your pastor the most when he or she is preparing a sermon or Bible study.

... *Through Worship and Growing with Other Believers*

It is only when men begin to worship that they begin to grow.
—Calvin Coolidge

▰▰▰

You should not stay away from the church meetings, as some are doing, but you should meet together and encourage each other.
(Hebrews 10:25, NCV)

I Can Barely Stay Awake

I probably would have fallen asleep in church last week. What saved me was Mrs. Thompson's stomach growling. We were five rows behind her and could hear it as if we were sitting right next to her. I went from barely staying awake to trying as hard as I could not to burst out laughing.

Sound familiar? Read on. Maybe the others will too.

Sunday School is boring. I like our teacher and all. Mrs. Davis is nice. But we don't talk about things that are interesting for teenagers.

Thomas:

I just finished high school this year. I go to college in the fall. There was a time when nobody thought I had a chance. I was in trouble a lot. I got into fights. I was angry, so I was always starting something. I took drugs quite a bit, and I was sexually active. At one point, I was sent to a juvenile detention center by a judge for about four months. I only got worse. My parents couldn't control me, and they really weren't there for me. Then I met a guy named Orlando. His dad was real strict, but he took an interest in me. He came to all our games, and he cheered for me as if I was his son. He took Orlando and me to professional games and all sorts of places. Then he invited me to their church. I got saved there. Orlando's dad led me through Bible studies. He prayed with me. He and his whole family basically changed my life. I'm going to school to be a pastor, and I've made a promise I'm going to help kids as Orlando's dad helped me

The pastor only talks to the adults in his sermons. He doesn't understand me and my friends.

I wish my parents would stop making me go on Wednesday nights. It's just one more service. Besides, I'm tired after school, and I end up missing my favorite TV show.

One of the best ways for you to spend time with God is through the services at your church and through spending time with other believers. When we commit ourselves to worship, God commits himself to being there with us. When we pray together with other Christians, there is a special power available through such united prayer. When we study the Bible together at Sunday School or a Wednesday night meeting, we are hearing not only our human teacher and the words of others but also the very teaching of God.

However, how many times do we fail to really show up for this meeting with God? How many times is our body there, while our attention and heart are in an entirely different location? Do we have a habit of "standing God up"?

To us, church is often a place to see friends and get out of the house, but it's not always a place to have a special meeting with God.

Church *should* be a place to see friends and have fun. It is great to socialize and meet with friends there. However, we might be on weaker ground when we demand that the pastor needs to change his sermons and that we need a new Sunday School teacher in order for it to be spiritually profitable and interesting. There are some things *you* need to do if worship and times with other believers are to be special times spent with God!

Expectation, Preparation, and Concentration

Often our presence in the services of the church is not the special meeting with God that it is intended to be because we lack one or all of the following three conditions:

1. Expectation

Expectations are a powerful force in our lives. It is no mystery that quite often what we expect or what others expect from us is exactly what we get.

If you expect to get good grades, you have a much better chance of getting good grades than if you do not expect to do so.

If someone is told long enough and often enough that he or she is stupid, there will come a point when he or she believes that. It doesn't matter how intelligent or unintelligent the person actually is. He or she *expects* to be stupid; his or her performance now reflects that expectation.

What do you expect out of the services at your church? Do you expect to experience God in a profound way? Do you expect to learn truths that will revolutionize your life? Or do you expect to be bored and to barely hang in there?

The way that you answer these questions will in large part determine what you get out of church.

2. Preparation

Perhaps more Sunday morning sermons are ruined by late-night Saturdays than by any other cause. Many of your friends—plus a lot of adults—miss out tremendously on the services of Sunday due to their Saturday night habits. There's nothing wrong with wanting to have fun with your friends on the weekend and wanting to stay up late. That's perfectly natural. However, you might want to designate Friday as your really late night to goof around. Try not to expend all of your energy on Saturday night. Don't ignore the needs of your body; prepare yourself physically so that you're not exhausted on Sunday morning.

Other preparation factors include obvious things such as homework. We are told that one day is to be set aside specifically for rest and for the Lord: the Sabbath. It is difficult to do so when you are worrying about the physics problems you never started and the history report on Andrew Jackson that needs to be finished before Monday morning.

Are you saying I can never do homework on Sunday?

Many have found that refraining from work on Sunday frees them up for needed spiritual and physical renewal. They have also found that the other six days of the week go much better and are much more productive by doing so. Can you ever do homework on Sunday? Sure, if you must. But a good way to prepare for Sunday is to finish homework by Saturday.

Different churches meet on different days. The question is: have you truly set aside a time of "Sabbath" for worship, fellowship, and rest?

The most important preparation you can do to make Sunday a special meeting time with God is the preparation you do in your heart. Before going to church and meeting with other Christians to worship, you need to express to God:

▶ **your need to meet with Him in a special way**
▶ **your willingness to open your heart to whatever He wants to say to you**
▶ **your desire to become more Christlike**
▶ **your desire to praise and honor Him**

When you expect to meet with God and when you prepare yourself to meet with Him, you need only one more condition to make the very most of this time:

3. Concentration

All throughout high school and college I played the strange and wonderful sport of tennis for my school teams. I discovered through my wins and losses that physical abilities are only part of what determines the outcome of a match. On occasion I would beat a player who I thought was more skilled than I. But I also lost to players I thought I was better than.

What was the difference? Mental concentration.

The worship service and other services of the church really are a time to be with God. You need to find ways to close out the distractions and focus on Him. But be careful that you don't concentrate so much on shutting out the distractions that you still aren't focusing on God.

Concentration is further complicated by the fact that we live in a media-bombarded society. Many of us are so bonded to TV that we truly have become couch potatoes. If we aren't in front of a TV or computer screen, then at least the radio is on. Though TV and other media are not necessarily evil, they certainly can take away from our ability to concentrate. TV in particular is so absorbing that it becomes more difficult to expend the needed energy to connect to other forms of communication.

Is it any wonder that we go to church and feel as if we didn't meet with God? It's difficult to tune in. That is one of the reasons camps and retreats are so valuable. Maybe while on a retreat or at a camp, you have said, or heard someone else say, something like, "I can't believe how close to God I got this week. I really sensed His presence. And when I go back home, I want to take this feeling with me."

Why did you sense God's presence so keenly at a camp or retreat? You went somewhere where there was probably no TV. Radios might have been outlawed. There may have been certain mandated quiet times. You sensed God in a special way. At camp you were helped to get rid of enough distractions that you were able to concentrate and see the God who is always there—at camp *and* at home!

What this means is that you may have to cultivate the ability to concentrate while in a worship service or a Bible study. You may have to work at finding helps to better tune in to what God is wanting to say to you.

Take a minute now to evaluate yourself in the areas of expectation, preparation, and concentration. Then set some growth goals in these areas.

When it comes to what I expect out of church, I usually . . .

___ *Expect nothing—which is what I get.*

___ *Expect to meet with God—and do!*

When it comes to preparing to meet God through worship . . .

___ *I sometimes cram at the very last minute.*

___ *I take time to search my heart and ask God to speak to me.*

When it comes to concentrating during worship services . . .

___ *I do better at hangman and writing notes to friends.*

___ *I tune in to the scripture and the pastor's message.*

Some Ways I Can Grow

One tool to help you in the areas of expectation, preparation, and concentration is your journal, helping you focus on what is really happening. Use this space to record:

—a brief prayer, asking God to meet with you in a special way

—needs in your congregation for you to remember in prayer

—notes from the Word of God that your pastor shares

—ways the message applies to you

Why All This Fuss?

Really. Isn't this a lot of trouble? Do I really need to do all that writing in a journal to worship God?

Of course you don't need to fill out a journal in order to worship God and grow with other believers. Your journal is simply a tool. For many, writing notes and keeping up a journal during worship helps them focus on what God wants to say to them. It helps them prepare and concentrate. If this isn't the case with you, remember what was said in the opening chapter. The goal is not to fill in a journal but to spend time with God.

61

Through Worship and Growing . . .

Here are two important reminders about worship and other ways to grow with other believers.

1. Worship is expressing our love for God.

Jesus told a lawyer who wanted to know what the greatest commandment was: "'Love the Lord your God with all your heart and with all your soul and with all your mind.' This is the first and greatest commandment" (Matthew 22:37-38).

At the heart of worship is our expression of love for God. We need to come together to honor Him with praise and thanksgiving—the first two attitudes of our personal prayer life. That is why we sing, read Scripture, and pray together. As a Body of Believers, we unite in praise and thanksgiving to God.

Worship is also a time to remember God's great act of redemption in our lives. That is why we celebrate Communion together on a regular basis. Paul reminds us: "The Lord Jesus, on the night he was betrayed, took bread, and when he had given thanks, he broke it and said, 'This is my body, which is for you; do this in remembrance of me.' In the same way, after supper he took the cup, saying, 'This cup is the new covenant in my blood; do this, whenever you drink it, in remembrance of me.' For whenever you eat this bread and drink this cup, you proclaim the Lord's death until he comes" (1 Corinthians 11:23-26).

Worship is to be done with other believers. In previous chapters we have focused more on our alone times with God. Though there should be many times of personal worship in your life, you also need to come together with other believers to worship. Throughout the Old and New Testaments the community of believers is called to come together to worship God over and over again.

2. Worship is also a time when we acknowledge God's claim on our lives.

That is why we so strongly stress the preaching of the Word. We believe that ministers don't just tell us about God, but that through the empowering of the Holy Spirit, God speaks directly to us through the sermon!

The worship service also prepares us to go out into the world to serve. The second part of Jesus' words to the lawyer continued: "And the second [commandment] is like it: 'Love your neighbor as yourself.' All the Law and the Prophets hang on these two commandments" (Matthew 22:39-40). Worship and adoration of God result in a renewed love and service toward others. In worship, we are scattered throughout the world and throughout our cities to serve, but then we gather again to glorify God. When we worship Him in this way, we are strengthened to scatter again for another week, renewed to be salt in our world.

We Can't Make It on Our Own

In Hebrews 10:25, we read this powerful admonition: "Let us not give up meeting together, as some are in the habit of doing, but let us encourage one another—and all the more as you see the Day approaching."

We are to worship together, and we are to find other ways to grow together with other Christians. Though salvation is a personal decision all of us must make by our own choosing, we must never forget that Christians need each other. In 1 Corinthians 12, Paul describes the church as a body. Though every part is different, each part is needed. What is a body without two eyes? Two ears? A mouth? Two hands? Two feet? What is your church without you? It is less than it could be!

You need the church, and the church needs you. Here are some relationships with her and her people you should pursue:

1. Small groups

Whether you get with a small group during a regularly scheduled sharing time on Sunday, Wednesday night, or in someone's home another night of the week, this is a tremendous way to spend time with God and grow closer to Him. All you do is find several other friends who will take a pledge with you to keep each other growing. The advantage of a small support group is that there is built-in accountability. Everyone in the group knows each other and is comfortable together. This allows for more opportunities to share needs and temptations and to receive needed support from the others in the group.

You can design small groups to include Bible study, intercessory prayer, and fellowship. You can use the work from other parts of your journal as you meet together.

2. Family devotions

You mean some families have devotions together?

Yes! When you consider others who can link up with you to provide mutual Christian support, don't forget your family! If your family already has devotions and prayer together, thank God for the love that shows. If not, is there a way you could suggest to Mom or Dad (assuming that they are Christians) that maybe the family needs a special time each day or week when Scripture is read, values are discussed, and you all pray for each other? Obviously, this isn't an option in many homes, and if that's the case with you, let this serve as a reminder to pray for your family.

If your family doesn't attend church and worship together, don't forget younger brothers and sisters. Could you be the one to read them a Bible story and say a prayer with them at night?

3. Prayer partners

Consider finding one other person for whom and with whom you agree to pray every day. You may or may not be able to meet with this person on a regular basis outside of church, but you keep in contact enough to let each other know that prayers for one another are continuing.

4. Bible study groups

The two most common times of Bible study for teenagers in many churches are Wednesday nights and during Sunday School. Take advantage of these times to learn God's Word. Go with the attitude that you will contribute and participate in the study. Be ready to dig in and discover insights for your own life and the lives of others. Remember, your expectations will determine to a large degree what you get out of—and put into—this time!

Many junior highs and high schools now allow voluntary prayer or Bible study groups to meet before school officially starts or after it ends. Are you the student leader who needs to get something started in your school?

5. A mentor

If the term *mentor* seems strange to you, it is because this is a relationship that is not practiced in our culture very often. You remember Paul's relationship with Timothy, don't you? He considered Timothy a son. He was there to teach and support Timothy during his youth.

Is there someone in your church who could serve as a mentor to you? Someone who would be willing to listen when you have problems and need advice? Someone who will help you stay true to your commitment to be a follower of Jesus Christ?

It could be that you and your parents have a very close relationship, and most of the mentoring will come from them. That's terrific. Thank God for such a blessing. Don't take for granted such a positive situation. However, if you are feeling the need for more support, consider talking to someone in your church about being an adopted spiritual father or mother to you!

6. Fellowship

Don't forget that having fun and being a Christian go hand in hand! In fact, Christian teenagers can have the greatest fun and fellowship together. Why? The self-destructive practices that are a part of so many teens' social lives are not needed for a good time. Whether it is a scheduled teen activity or having other Christians over to your house, you will benefit from spending time with people who share your values and commitments.

Your Reactions and Actions

1. Can you think of the names of two or three people your age that might be interested in forming a support group with you?

2. What is your main motivation for going to church right now?
   ___ My parents make me go.
   ___ I want to spend time with friends.
   ___ I want to grow as a Christian.
   ___ (Other) _____

3. What are some ways you can prepare right now for next Sunday's worship service?

4. Read Isaiah 6. In what ways is Isaiah's experience what a worship service should be like?

5. Spend a moment in silent prayer, asking God to bless your pastor and others who will help lead the upcoming service at your church.

STWG...

7

... Through Ministering to Others

I expect to pass through life but once. If therefore, there be any kindness I can show, or any good thing I can do to any fellow being, let me do it now, and not defer or neglect it, as I shall not pass this way again.
—William Penn

Whoever wants to become great among you must be your servant.
(Mark 10:43)

This Is a Test!

1. If you could do only one of the following two options, which would you choose?

   a. Go to Hawaii with your family for an all-expenses-paid vacation.

   b. Spend a week at a homeless shelter serving meals and helping take care of children.

2. If you had $250 in a savings account, what would you prefer to do with the cash?

   a. Spend an evening at the mall, giving your wardrobe a serious makeover.

   b. Put the money toward a special teen project to help our church's Compassionate Ministries offering.

Sandy:
I went with my youth group to help this church in a really bad part of town. We got a music and puppet program ready. We thought we would help the kids in the neighborhood a lot. And we did. They were so hungry for love that they loved being with us. But I discovered that the person who changed the most was me. God really got hold of my life that week. I don't want to ever be the same selfish person I was before. I want to make a real difference in my world.

3. When you finish your schooling, which job would you prefer?
   a. Working as a business executive, making a very big salary.
   b. Serving as a missionary in a third world country on a very limited income.

4. If you went to a pizza shop with a friend after school, what would you prefer to talk about?
   a. The person you'd like to start dating.
   b. What the Lord has done in your life recently.

5. If you walked in the school cafeteria, with whom would you rather sit?
   a. A group of your friends whom you sit with every day.
   b. A new student who is slightly out of it, and who is sitting by himself for the seventh day in a row.

6. After taking this test, do you feel that the author of this book is:
   a. Trying to make you feel guilty.
   b. Asking perhaps the easiest test questions you have ever had in your life.
   c. Leading up to something else.

The correct answers to numbers 1 through 5 are, of course, whichever answers you chose.

The correct answer to number 6 is, from my perspective, c.

I really don't want you to feel guilty if you chose a every single time without batting an eyelash. I hope, however, that these were not the most easy questions you have been asked in your life. I hope that even if you didn't give the other options a second thought as you chose Hawaii, the spending spree, the high-paying job, the conversation about the person you want to date, and the group of friends to sit with, that deep down you struggled with these questions just a little.

You must be kidding? Haven't you seen posters of Hawaii?

I have seen posters of Hawaii. Which brings us to answer c. Yes, this is really leading up to something.

Lord, We Want to Serve You!

In a passage from Mark's account of the gospel (10:35-45), we read that James and John, the sons of Zebedee, asked Jesus if they could have seats of honor in His kingdom, one at His right and the other at His left. This ambitious request came while Jesus and His disciples were making their final approach to Jerusalem—and nearing Jesus' death.

James and John were sure He was about to seize control of the city and establish His political and military kingdom. Even though Jesus had previously warned them that He must suffer and die, they could not come to grips with this fact.

If they had, they would have had no trouble being on Jesus' right and left hand—

▶ As He prayed in Gethsemane, instead of falling asleep a short distance off

▶ As He was led to His trial before the Jewish Sanhedrin, instead of keeping a safe distance, lost somewhere in a large city

▶ As He was handed over to Pilate, instead of fleeing the area with the other disciples

▶ As He was mocked and beaten by the cruel Roman soldiers, instead of hiding in the city

▶ As He hung on the Cross, instead of giving these places to two thieves. John watched from the front row, and James never showed up.

What these two fiery sons of Zebedee didn't understand is the same thing we struggle to understand: "The greatest among you will be your servant. For whoever exalts himself will be humbled, and whoever humbles himself will be exalted" (Matthew 23:11-12). Jesus' standard of greatness is servanthood. Are you willing to:

—build others up in the Body of Christ, even when you don't feel as if you are getting all the attention you deserve?

—look after other people's needs before your own?

—show compassion and demonstrate love to those less fortunate than yourself?

—persistently do good works?

"Isn't This Book About 'Spending Time with God'?"

Aren't you getting off the subject of this book? I can read about service somewhere else. I want to know more about developing a devotional life and spending time with God. I thought this book was about spending time with God.

Usually we think of time with God as our quiet time, our journaling time, our time set aside for prayer and worship. We don't think of raking our neighbor's yard as spending time with God—unless, of course, we pray while we are working.

But one of the most effective ways that we can spend time with God in a special way is when we minister to others in His name. If actions really do speak louder than words, then some of our greatest prayers to God will be expressed when we love others in tangible ways.

The two greatest commandments, according to Jesus, are to love God with everything we've got and to love our neighbor as ourselves. Our neighbor is anybody with a need with whom we come into contact.

The starting point in all this is a servant attitude. In life, at your school, at every level of society, there are givers and takers. Some—the givers—see what they can do for others. Some—the takers—see what they can get out of others.

As a follower of Jesus Christ, you will always be a taker, because you have received redemption through Jesus' blood. But you are also called to be a giver, someone who passes on what God has done in his or her life.

What follows are some obvious ways that you can be a servant of Jesus Christ through ministry to others. Each of these ways could be dealt with in an entire book, and in many cases they have been. So don't expect a complete how-to in each area. But if you are willing to be a servant, and if you are ready to plan some ways to express that servant attitude, you're off to a tremendous start!

Ways to Minister to Others

1. Compassionate ministries

"Then the righteous will answer him, 'Lord, when did we see you hungry and feed you, or thirsty and give you something to drink? When did we see you a stranger and invite you in, or needing clothes and clothe you? When did we see you sick or in prison and go to visit you?'

"The King will reply, 'I tell you the truth, whatever you did for one of the least of these brothers of mine, you did for me'" (Matthew 25:37-40).

These verses are just part of a powerful section of Scripture where Jesus teaches us how ministry to others is a ministry to Him. Notice that when we act with compassion to "the least," those in need, we are actually acting with compassion toward Jesus. When we feed the hungry, we are feeding Jesus.

The question is, are we feeding Jesus enough to fill Him up, or are we letting Him go hungry because we don't have enough scraps left over from our abundant dinners?

There are many ways you can practice a compassionate ministry of feeding "the hungry":

▶ **You can get involved in district and local church projects that involve ministry to the needy.**

▶ You can give money to and help raise money for missionary efforts and other special offerings that meet needs.

▶ You can prepare now for missionary service or for a year or two of volunteer service when you are done with school.

There are also many closer-to-home and less spectacular ways to minister to the needy. Is there someone in your teen group or at your school who is lonely and friendless? Are you willing to meet this person's need by being a friend? Go back to question 5 at the beginning of this chapter. Would you be willing to choose *b* from time to time in order to minister to that person—and to Jesus?

Let's keep your goals for this section close to home for now. Is there someone in your teen group or at your school who is "the least of these"? What can you do to minister to that person right now?

2. Building up other believers

Everyone needs to belong and feel accepted. If you don't accept me and make me feel welcome over a long enough period of time, I will go somewhere else to find acceptance. The need to belong is basic to being a human.

We in the church are no different. We need to belong. And if *we* need this, so do others. That means that we must minister to others through helping them belong. We cannot just talk about loving each other; we need to practice it.

Why do people leave churches? Studies show that among teenagers and adults, most go somewhere else because they did not feel loved and accepted where they were. Cults recruit many new members from Christian churches. Despite the strange teachings of these groups, many people join anyway. Why? Because they are truly cared for and shown that they are wanted and needed by the members of the cult.

Acceptance is, of course, a two-way street. There are some teenagers who don't fit into a church youth group, not because others don't welcome them but because they refuse to let others get close and don't seem to want to belong. The point is, you must be willing to take the first step, and the second step, and the third step, and whatever other steps you feel God would want you to take. But you won't always be successful in including others.

Near the end of His earthly ministry, Jesus shared these words with His disciples: "A new command I give you: Love one another. As I have loved you, so you must love one another. By this all men will know that you are my disciples, if you love one another" (John 13:34-35).

Two truths jump out from this passage. First, if we hope to have a testimony to the world, we inside the church must love each other. People who don't have a personal relationship with Jesus Christ will know that we truly follow Him when we truly love each other. The second truth is that if we want to love Jesus and obey Him, we must love other Christians and find ways to demonstrate that love. Jesus loved with words and actions. His is the model we are to follow.

There are other avenues of building up other believers in your church than just that of reaching out to the friends who are close to your age. There may be senior adults who need help with shopping or simply need someone to visit and read to them. There may be young adults who occasionally need a teen to call them and say, "If you want to go out sometime, I would be happy to come over and baby-sit your children for free." There may be a VBS class to help with this summer and a host of other ways you can minister to the people in your church.

Write down two or three ways that you can help build the Body of Believers in your church!

3. Through consistent kindness and good deeds

Compassion and kindness should not be seen as things to do out of duty. We need to build a lifestyle of kindness and good deeds, not with a spirit of superiority—"Yeah, I guess I'll help some people out who aren't as lucky as me"—but with a spirit of servanthood. Scripture is full of commands that remind us to live and love as givers.

"Carry each other's burdens, and in this way you will fulfill the law of Christ" (Galatians 6:2).

"Let us not become weary in doing good, for at the proper time we will reap a harvest if we do not give up" (v. 9).

"Show me your faith without deeds, and I will show you my faith by what I do" (James 2:18).

The list of scriptures goes on and on. The list of ways to be a minister goes on and on also. Don't limit yourself to what has been written in this book. Find other ways to love God by loving others. Don't settle for a Christian experience that is all talk and no action. For in reality, that is not a true Christian experience. If you truly want to love God, one of the key ways you do so is to love other people!

Create a Spending Time with God Plan

The source of your strength and the key to your ministry is the Holy Spirit. The Holy Spirit provides us with gifts and power to carry out our ministry to others. But the Holy Spirit does not *force* us to minister to others. He *calls* us to minister to others. That means we must respond to that calling. The way to begin responding is to make plans to minister. As with the other activities, ministry to others will not happen by accident. You must do it on purpose.

Use your journal to help you plan your ministry to others.

Once a week, perhaps on Sunday afternoon or Monday morning, when you can look ahead to what is coming up at school, at church, and in the other areas of your life, write down ways you can make a difference in your world.

At the end of the week, list what you were able to do—right across from the ministry goals you recorded. The reason for you to fill in what you actually did is not so that you will feel guilty if you didn't do everything on your list. It's so that you can regularly evaluate your ministry to others:

Am I keeping a servant attitude? Am I sensitive to the others in my teen group? Am I showing God's love to my neighbors?

It will also remind you to rewrite the names of people to whom you didn't get a chance to minister in the past week, but to whom you do want to reach out this next week.

Your Reactions and Actions

1. Read James 2:14-19. At this point in your life, are you living out what James is calling for? Why, or why not?

2. Read Romans 12:4-8. Do you recognize any of these gifts in your life? Which one(s)? Why? (If you don't recognize any of these gifts, can you think of another spiritual gift that

God has given you?) Write out ways God can minister through you.

3. Can you think of a ministry project that you and the other teens from your church could attempt? What can you do to help make this happen?

4. Why don't you call your pastor to see if there is a ministry in the church that you might be able to fulfill. If he or she does not have something that comes immediately to mind, let him or her know you are willing to serve as opportunities arise.

... *Through Sharing Your Faith*

I have now disposed of all my property to my family. There is one thing more I wish I could give them, and that is the Christian religion. If they had that, and I had not given them one shilling, they would have been rich; and if they had not that, and I had given them all the world, they would be poor.
—Patrick Henry

▚▲▲▲▟

How, then, can they call on the one they have not believed in? And how can they believe in the one of whom they have not heard? And how can they hear without someone preaching to them?
(Romans 10:14)

The Edge of the Ledge

I was 17 years old, driving through the Great Smoky Mountains on family vacation. We all hit the saturation point, where at the same time everyone feels an intense claustrophobia and has to get out of the car. Just off the road ahead there was a clearing beside a cool Tennessee stream with about 10 cars

Hunter:
I don't know where I would be without Shannon. She's the one who told me about Jesus Christ. We were both only 13 at the time. We lived three houses apart and had grown up together and been best friends as long as I can remember. My family didn't really go to church. Maybe once or twice a year. But it wasn't a big deal for us. So my parents didn't mind when I went to church camps with her each summer, and then started going to her church every week when we went into sixth grade. I liked all the people. But it wa Shannon, my best friend, who really helped me know what it means to have a relationship with God. She's the one who prayed with me. Now m mom and little sister are Christians too! We're working on my dad. I pray for him every nig

parked there—we must not have been the only ones who came down with a bad case of claustrophobia. Just about 10 yards farther down, the stream turned into a pool. Thirty-three feet above the pool was a ledge that was perfectly situated for diving.

I decided I had to dive the 33 feet into the pool. Maybe I was feeling the need to prove my manhood. That's a major issue at age 17. I confidently climbed up the path that led to the edge. And I confidently walked to the edge. Then I looked down. I suddenly didn't want to jump anymore. The problem is that about 25 people, including my family, and especially my two sisters, had already watched me walk up the path—and knew my intention. To back down now would be to lose face—no way to prove your manhood. Well, it wasn't a pretty sight. But after about five minutes of mustering my courage, with my heart pounding, I dove.

You would think I learned my lesson. But I found myself in a similar predicament several years later when I went sky-diving for the first time. Yes, I managed to get out of the plane. But barely.

How about you? Are you on the edge of the ledge too? I'm not talking about a 33-foot dive into a cool Tennessee spring or jumping out of an airplane.

Have you come to the point in your life where you feel it is time to start sharing your faith with friends? When you think about telling someone what Jesus Christ has done in your life, do you feel as I did, perched on the edge of the edge? Maybe now it's time to take the plunge.

Because one of the ways we spend time with God is to tell others just what He's done for us through Jesus Christ.

Overcoming the Fear of Sharing

Perhaps no other area of ministry produces as much fear in us as witnessing. Does it really make you nervous to share about Jesus with someone who does not have a personal relationship with God? Why?

Are you afraid the person might reject or misunderstand you?

Are you afraid you will forget what to say?

Here are some suggestions others have given me that have helped take away my fear of witnessing. These commonsense suggestions will undoubtedly help you feel more free to witness also!

Some guidelines on sharing your faith with others include:

1. Realize that witnessing begins by building relationships with others.

Some Christians are able to witness to people they don't know very well or at all, because they are able to establish an immediate rapport. I was at a conference in downtown Chicago and took a cab ride with a man who ministers in the inner city of Milwaukee. He is about 6'9" and weighs around 350 pounds. You could describe him as a "gentle giant." He's never met a stranger in his life. In less than 15 minutes of riding in a cab, he had asked the driver about his life and whether he had a relationship with God. He went on to tell him about how much Jesus loved him. He asked if he could pray with him. The driver, who spoke broken English, bowed his head and prayed to accept Jesus right outside the convention center.

Amazing! Most of us cannot do this. Or at least we haven't had the courage to try. If you are someone who has "never met a stranger" in your life, though, I certainly don't want to discourage you from this type of witnessing.

Most of us, however, will truly be most effective in witnessing to those with whom we have already built relationships. There is a reason for this. It has to do with how others receive the gospel. When it comes to something as important as your religious faith, *people don't care what you know until they know that you care.*

The scary part is that they'll ask questions about you in their mind.

Do you live what you preach? Is there something different about your life? Is there something in the way you live that they would like to have also?

These questions will most often come up as you build bridges to other people. This does not mean that you get close to others just so you can witness to them. They might feel used. But as you do get close to others, you will open up doors of opportunity to witness.

One caution: Do keep in mind that the people to whom you are the closest will have a tremendous influence in your life. Though you need to build relationships with non-Christian friends if you are going to be salt in your world, don't forget that you need a strong core of Christian friends to help create the positive peer pressure that should be a part of your life. This is part of the creative tension of being "in the world [but] not of the world" (John 17:13-16).

2. Know clearly what God has done for you.

This means that you should always be ready to present a testimony of what God has done and is doing in your life. Your testimony should include:

- ◐ your life before you became a Christian
- ◐ how you became a Christian
- ◐ your life after you became a Christian
- ◐ what God means to you right now

Think through your testimony, so that when you present it to someone, you can do so confidently. The best way to do this is to write out your salvation story. You would never want to read it to someone to whom you were witnessing, but this will help you anchor it in your mind. Use your journal to record your personal salvation story.

3. Be sensitive to opportunities to witness to others.

Sometimes it is better not to witness to someone than it is to witness. Why? You might sense a strong barrier in his or her life that needs to be broken down before you will be effective. You might sense that he or she is not tuned in to what you are saying at a given moment. You might sense that he or she is simply not ready right now.

Be sensitive to the person, and even more so to the Holy Spirit. It is the Holy Spirit who brings conviction into others' lives. That means *we* don't have to convince people of their sins; that is the Spirit's job. You only need to be sensitive to the Spirit's leading in your own life. Keep up-to-date in your prayer life. Ask for guidance. This does not ensure success every time you witness, because each person must decide for himself or herself whether he or she will accept Jesus Christ. But such sensitivity to the Holy Spirit and to others will help you witness at the time when they are most open and receptive to the message of the gospel.

4. Know the heart of the gospel message, and be able to present it in a way the person can understand.

One witnessing tool that many Christians have found effective is a simple outline based on the theme: Life Can Have True Meaning. The main points are listed below. Take some time to learn the major ideas and scriptures for this or another gospel presentation.

Don't forget that such a presentation is most effective with someone with whom you've already built a relationship—and after you have shared your personal testimony.

Life Can Have True Meaning

Once you become acquainted with the following outline, begin to put it into your own words. Again, remember that people won't care what you know until they know that you care. It has to come from your heart.

Begin by asking: Have you ever wondered what the true meaning of your life is? Why you are here? If your life truly matters?

The good news is that God can give your life incredible meaning. I know He has given my life meaning I never knew before. May I share how I know your life has meaning?

Step 1

God loves you and has a plan for your life.
- —His love is for everyone—and specifically includes you (John 3:16).
- —Because of His love, God offers you a life of abundance, a life filled with meaning (John 10:10).

Step 2

Sin separates you from God and from others.
- —Everyone who has ever lived—even the "holiest" person you have ever met—has sinned (Romans 3:23).
- —Sin brings spiritual death (Romans 6:23).
- —Our own efforts to be good and live right cannot save us (Ephesians 2:8-9).

Step 3

Jesus Christ died and rose again for our sins.
- —Even though we deserved to die for our sins, Jesus died in our place (Romans 5:8).
- —Jesus Christ is the Way to this remarkable new life (2 Corinthians 5:17).
- —Jesus gives us a sense of meaning and inner peace (Romans 5:1).
- —Jesus gives us freedom from the sin that has messed up our lives and killed our spirit (John 8:36).
- —Jesus gives us the amazing gift of eternal life—of living forever with God (Romans 6:23).

Step 4

You must repent and ask God for forgiveness.
- —Admit and confess your sins to God (Proverbs 28:13).

- Repentance means
  - ◐ you are ready to acknowledge your sins
  - ◐ you are now sorry for your sins
  - ◐ you confess your sins
  - ◐ you are willing and ready to walk away from your sins
  - ◐ your life is changed by Christ
- Forgiveness is one of God's most special promises to us (1 John 1:9).

Step 5

Place your trust in Christ and receive Him as your Savior.
- Christ is ready to come into your life right now (Revelation 3:20).
- You need to receive Him now (John 1:12).

What to pray:

Lord Jesus, I want to have life. I know that I have sinned. I need Your forgiveness and pardon. I believe that You died and rose again for my sins. I now accept You as my personal Savior. I will forsake my sinful life. I know that Your grace and power will enable me to live for You. Thank You, Jesus, for saving me and for giving me a new life.

The joy you will feel when you walk through the steps of salvation with a friend or family member is incredible. Not only will they be changed, but your life will never be the same either.

5. Learn to witness from others.

What you have read here is so brief that you will want to pursue further opportunities to learn to witness. Perhaps your church has a personal evangelism program. Ask your pastor if you can go on personal evangelism calls with someone who is experienced and who can show you better what to expect and to do.

A Spending Time with God Prayer

Dear God,

We praise You right now as we draw near to You. You are a good God, a gracious and loving God.

Thank You for Your incredible love for us; for the way You want to have a relationship with us; for the way You are at work to make us into the persons You want us to become.

Help each of us to know You better. Sometimes we have become so caught up in our own problems and all the activities of our lives that we have forgotten that You are there. Forgive us. We are ready now to spend time with You.

We know that all our needs will be met by You. We don't have to worry. So we bring all the concerns of our lives to You.

Not everyone acknowledges and knows You, God. We pray for our family, our friends, and our acquaintances, that they will experience Your love and forgiveness in their lives.

All this we pray in Jesus' name. Amen.

Your Reactions and Actions

1. Is there a friend at school whom you would like to help lead into a relationship with Christ? Write his or her name in the space below, and follow it with a prayer, asking God to help you find—and make—an opportunity to witness.

   Name: _____
   Prayer:

2. Who is the person who most helped you to know Jesus Christ? Have you ever thanked that person? Why not write a letter to him or her now.

3. Write out your testimony. You might want to open your journal now and write it there.